MEXICO

Waiting for Justice
in Chiapas

Physicians for Human Rights
&
Human Rights Watch/Americas

Physicians for Human Rights
Boston • San Francisco

Library of Congress Catalog Card No. 94-068655
ISBN: 1-879707-17-9

Cover design: Glenn Ruga/Visual Communications

Cover photo: *In the ejido of Morelia, the wives of Severiano
Santiz Gómez, Sebastián Santiz López, and Hermelindo Santiz
Gómez are still waiting for the Mexican government to identify and
prosecute the military personnel responsible for the torture and
murder of their husbands. Army troops detained the three men on
January 7, 1994 (see Chapter VI). Five weeks later, their
partially skeletonized remains were found in a ravine near
Morelia. The remains were positively identified through
anthropological and DNA analysis.*

PHYSICIANS FOR HUMAN RIGHTS

Physicians for Human Rights (PHR) is an organization of health professionals, scientists, and concerned citizens which uses the knowledge and skills of the medical and forensic sciences to investigate and prevent violations of international human rights and humanitarian law.

Since 1986, PHR members have worked to stop torture, disappearances, and political killings by governments and opposition groups; to improve health and sanitary conditions in prisons and detention centers; to investigate the physical and psychological consequences of violations of humanitarian law in internal and international conflicts; to defend medical neutrality and the right of civilians and combatants to receive medical care during times of war; to protect health professionals who are victims of violations of human rights; and to prevent medical complicity in torture and other abuses.

PHR conducts educational and training projects for health professionals, members of the judiciary, and human rights advocates on the application of medical and forensic skills in the investigation of violations of human rights. PHR bases its actions on the Universal Declaration of Human Rights and other international human rights and humanitarian agreements. The organization adheres to a policy of strict impartiality and is concerned with the medical consequences of human rights abuses regardless of the ideology of the offending government or group.

Charles Clements, M.D., is President; Carola Eisenberg, M.D., is Vice President; Eric Stover is Executive Director; Susannah Sirkin is Deputy Director; Kari Hannibal is Membership and Education Coordinator; Gina VanderLoop is Development Director; Barbara Ayotte is Senior Program Associate; Shana Swiss, M.D., is Director of the Women's Program; Vincent Iacopino, M.D., is Western Regional Representative; and Clyde C. Snow, Ph.D., is Senior Forensic Consultant.

Physicians for Human Rights
100 Boylston Street, Suite 702
Boston, MA 02116 U.S.A.
Tel: (617) 695-0041
Fax: (617) 695-0307
E-mail: phrusa@igc.apc.org

Physicians for Human Rights
312 Sutter Street, Suite 606
San Francisco, CA 94108
Tel: (415) 765-6991
Fax: (415) 765-6993
E-mail: phrwro@igc.apc.org

HUMAN RIGHTS WATCH

Human Rights Watch conducts regular, systematic investigations of human rights abuses in some seventy countries around the world. It addresses the human rights practices of governments of all political stripes, of all geopolitical alignments, and of all ethnic and religious persuasions. In internal wars it documents violations by both governments and rebel groups. Human Rights Watch defends freedom of thought and expression, due process and equal protection of the law; it documents and denounces murders, disappearances, torture, arbitrary imprisonment, exile, censorship and other abuses of internationally recognized human rights.

Human Rights Watch began in 1978 with the founding of its Helsinki division. Today, it includes five divisions covering Africa, the Americas, Asia, the Middle East, as well as the signatories of the Helsinki accords. It also includes five collaborative projects on arms transfers, children's rights, free expression, prison conditions, and women's rights. It maintains offices in New York, Washington, Los Angeles, London, Brussels, Moscow, Belgrade, Zagreb, Dushanbe, and Hong Kong. Human Rights Watch is an independent, nongovernmental organization, supported by contributions from private individuals and foundations worldwide. It accepts no government funds, directly or indirectly.

The staff includes Kenneth Roth, executive director; Cynthia Brown, program director; Holly J. Burkhalter, advocacy director; Gara LaMarche, associate director; Juan Mendez, general counsel; Susan Osnos, communications director; and Derrick Wong, finance and administration director. The regional directors of Human Rights Watch are Abdullahi An-Na'im, Africa; Jose Miguel Vivanco, Americas; Sidney Jones, Asia; Jeri Laber, Helsinki; and Christopher E. George, Middle East. The project directors are Joost R. Hiltermann, Arms Project; Lois Whitman, Children's Rights Project; Gara LaMarche, Free Expression Project; Joanna Weschler, Prison Project; and Dorothy Q. Thomas, Women's Rights Project.

485 Fifth Avenue, New York, NY 10017-6104
Tel: (212) 972-8400, Fax: (212) 972-0905, E-mail: hrwatchnyc@igc.apc.org

1522 K Street, N.W., #910, Washington, DC 20005-1202
Tel: (202) 371-6592, Fax: (202) 371-0124, E-mail: hrwatchdc@igc.apc.org

10951 West Pico Blvd., #203, Los Angeles, CA 90064-2126
Tel: (310) 475-3070, Fax: (310) 475-5613, E-mail: hrwatchla@igc.apc.org

33 Islington High Street, N1 9LH London, UK
Tel: (71) 713-1995, Fax: (71) 713-1800, E-mail: hrwatchuk@gn.apc.org

Things are going to change in Mexico. We shall confront the new threats to human rights from wherever they come. The new social will and the aim of the reformed State is to adhere to the law...Let there be no doubt; the political line of the government of the Republic is to defend human rights and punish those who violate them; it is to end once and for all any kind of impunity.

President Carlos Salinas de Gortari, at the inaugural ceremony of the National Commission of Human Rights on June 6, 1990.

TABLE OF CONTENTS

GLOSSARY OF ACRONYMS

CCRI	Comité Clandestino Revolucionario Indígena (Clandestine Revolutionary Indian Committee)
CEOIC	Consejo Estatal de Organizaciones Indígenas y Campesinas (State Council of Indian and Peasant Organizations)
CNC	Confederación Nacional Campesina (National Peasant Confederation)
CNDH	Comisión Nacional de Derechos Humanos (National Commission of Human Rights)
CONPAZ	Coordinación de los Organismos no Gubernamentales de San Cristóbal de las Casas por la Paz (Coordinating Group for Nongovernmental Organizations Working for Peace in San Cristóbal de las Casas)
EZLN	Ejército Zapatista de Liberación Nacional (Zapatista National Liberation Army)
HRW/Americas	Human Rights Watch/Americas
ICRC	International Committee of the Red Cross
IFE	Instituto Federal Electoral (Federal Electoral Institute)

IMSS	Instituto Mexicano de Seguro Social (Mexican Social Security Institute)
INI	Instituto Nacional Indigenista (National Indigenous Institute)
MAHR	Minnesota Advocates for Human Rights
NAFTA	North American Free Trade Agreement
OCEZ	Organización Campesina Emiliano Zapata (Emiliano Zapata Peasant Organization)
PGJM	Procuraduría General de Justicia Militar (military Judicial Prosecutor's Office)
PGR	Procuraduría General de la República (federal Attorney General's office)
PHR	Physicians for Human Rights
PRD	Partido de la Revolución Democrática (Democratic Revolutionary Party)
PRI	Partido Revolucionario Institucional (Institutional Revolutionary Party)
SEDENA	Secretaría de Defensa Nacional (The Ministry of National Defense)
UAM	Universidad Autónoma Metropolitana (National Autonomous University of Mexico)

ACKNOWLEDGMENTS

This report was researched and written by Eric Stover (Executive Director, Physicians for Human Rights); Sebastian Brett (Consultant, Human Rights Watch/Americas); Thomas Crane, M.D. (Consultant, Physicians for Human Rights); and Clyde Collins Snow, Ph.D. (Senior Forensic Consultant, Physicians for Human Rights). Barbara Ayotte and Laura Reiner of Physicians for Human Rights prepared the manuscript for publication.

The report was reviewed by Cynthia Brown (Program Director, Human Rights Watch); Richard P. Claude, Ph.D. (Professor Emeritus of Government and Politics, University of Maryland); Robert H. Kirschner (Deputy Chief Medical Examiner, Cook County, Illinois); Anne Manuel (Associate Director, Human Rights Watch/Americas); and Susannah Sirkin (Deputy Director, Physicians for Human Rights).

We wish to thank the following persons for their assistance in preparing this report: Marcos Arana; Pedro Armendares; Margarita Arruza, M.D.; Ramona Bailley, M.D.; Anna Carrigan; Lucy Conger; Edith Demesa; Colin Hamblin; Luis Hernández; Marina Patricia Jiménez; Mary-Claire King, Ph.D.; Ellen Lutz; Roger Maldonado; Michael McCaughan; Lic. Monica Morales; Sor Patricia Moysen Marquez and the Vicentian nuns of the Hospital San Carlos; Liliana Nieto; Mercedes Osuna; Catherine Roberts; Father Pablo Romo; Sarah Rowell, Ph.D.; Saville Ryan; Susan Shaw; Morris Tidball Binz; and Barbara Trott, M.D. We are grateful for the invaluable assistance and information provided to us by several organizations, including the Centro de Derechos Humanos "Fray Bartolomé de las Casas"; Coordinación de Organismos No-Gubernamentales de Chiapas por la Paz; and Comisión Mexicana de Defensa y Promoción de los Derechos Humanos, A.C.

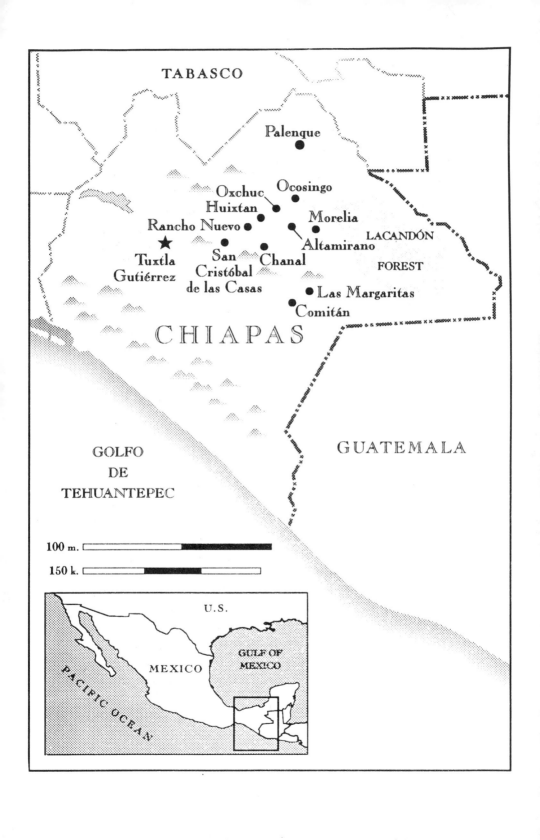

TABASCO

Palenque ●

Ocosingo
Oxchuc ●
Huixtan
Rancho Nuevo ● ● Morelia
★ ● Altamirano
Tuxtla San ● Chanal
Gutiérrez Cristóbal
de las Casas ● Las Margaritas
● Comitán

LACANDÓN

FOREST

CHIAPAS

GUATEMALA

GOLFO
DE
TEHUANTEPEC

100 m.

150 k.

U.S.

MEXICO

GULF OF
MEXICO

PACIFIC OCEAN

I. INTRODUCTION

Nineteen ninety-four has been a traumatic year for Mexico. The Indian uprising in the southeastern state of Chiapas which ushered in the New Year sent shock-waves across a nation confidently awaiting its entry into the North American Free Trade Agreement. In March, the presidential candidate of the ruling Institutional Revolutionary Party (PRI) was assassinated, a crime unprecedented in recent Mexican history. On August 21, Mexicans elected the PRI's replacement candidate, Ernesto Zedillo Ponce de León, who took office on December 1. Within weeks of Zedillo's victory, another high-ranking PRI official, José Francisco Ruiz Massieu, was gunned down in Mexico City.

As most Mexicans and the international press turned away from the rebellion in Chiapas to the presidential elections, Physicians for Human Rights (PHR) and Human Rights Watch/Americas (HRW/Americas) continued to investigate the violent events of the first two weeks of January 1994 (see Chapter VI). Our interest went beyond the alleged abuses themselves to examining the methods and procedures employed by three governmental agencies--the federal Attorney General's office (Procuraduría General de la República/PGR), the National Commission of Human Rights (Comisión Nacional de Derechos Humanos/CNDH), and the military Judicial Prosecutor's office (Procuraduría General de Justicia Militar/PGJM)--all of which were charged with investigating complaints of violations of human rights arising from the New Year's Day rebellion.

Our organizations believe that the Mexican government's commitment to ensure justice to the scores of citizens whose basic rights were violated during and after the conflict will be a litmus test of its declared intentions to take Mexico into a new era of respect for human rights. However, as this report documents, these aspirations are a long way from being realized.

On paper, Mexico is one of the most advanced countries with regard to the legal protection of human rights. The Mexican Constitution[1] and secondary legislation[2] provide explicit guarantees for the protection of human rights and individual freedoms. In addition to its obligations under the Universal Declaration of Human Rights, Mexico has ratified the International Covenant on Civil and Political Rights,[3] the Convention Against Torture or Other Cruel, Inhuman and

---

[1] The first chapter of the Mexican Constitution, including the first twenty-nine articles, is entitled "Concerning Individual Guarantees." Article 16 provides that no person may be disturbed in his person, family, domicile, papers or possessions unless by virtue of a written order by the competent authority stating the basis and legal grounds for the procedure. Article 19 states that any ill-treatment during arrest or confinement, all discomforts without legal justification, as well as any taxes or payments in the prisons, are abuses which shall be punishable by law and reprimanded by the authorities. Article 20 guarantees the right to a hearing within forty-eight hours of arrest.

[2] The federal Congress, pursuant to Article 73 of the Constitution, has promulgated the Penal Code for the Federal District which also applies to any federal court when the matter falls under federal jurisdiction. The federal and state penal codes describe several different kinds of criminal abuses of authority by public servants which are subject to punishment. In addition, the Federal Congress has enacted several special federal laws, such as the Federal Law to Prevent and Punish Torture, which establish certain federal crimes and their corresponding punishment. Ley Federal Para Prevenir y Sancionar la Tortura, D.O., May 27, 1986, Art. 1.

[3] International Covenant on Civil and Political Rights, December 16, 1966, GA res. 2200A (XXI), 21 UN GAOR, Supp. (No. 16) at 52, U.N. Doc. A/6316 (1966) entered into force March 23, 1976. Mexico acceded to the Covenant on March 23, 1981.

2

Degrading Treatment or Punishment,[4] and the American
Convention on Human Rights.[5]

In reality, the Mexican government lacks the political will
to enforce these protections. Today, scores of Chiapenecos are
waiting for justice. Some were tortured by military interrogators.
Others were widowed when soldiers detained and summarily
executed their husbands. Eyewitnesses can attest to these crimes.
And there is ample circumstantial and physical evidence to bring
charges against specific army officers who had command
responsibilities at the time these crimes were committed.

Now, nearly a year later, none of the cases of torture and
extrajudicial executions documented in this report has been
properly investigated, nor have any of those responsible for these
crimes been identified and held accountable. Investigations into
fatal excesses in the use of military firepower have been equally
unsatisfactory and inconclusive. Similarly, no court has objected
to the scores of arrests which were carried out without legal
authority and in violation of constitutional norms during the
conflict.

This report is based on research conducted in Chiapas by
representatives of HRW/Americas and PHR from January to June
1994. PHR retained Thomas Crane, M.D., a family physician
from Santa Rosa, California, as its representative in Chiapas from
January 1 to April 8. Ellen Lutz, former director of Human Rights

---

[4] The Convention Against Torture and Other Cruel, Inhuman or
Degrading Treatement or Punishment, December 10, 1984, GA res. 46
(XXXIX), 39 UN GAOR, Supp. (No. 51) p. 197, U.N. Doc. A/39/51
(1984) entered into force June 26, 1987. Mexico ratified the Convention
Against Torture on January 23, 1986.

[5] American Convention on Human Rights, November 22, 1969, OAS
Doc. OEA/Ser.L/V/II.65, doc. 6 (1985) entered into force July 18,
1978. Mexico acceded to the American Convention on Human Rights on
April 2, 1982.

Watch's California office, visited Chiapas from January 9 to 14. HRW/Americas research associate Sebastian Brett was there from February 8 to 16, and again from June 24 to 27. From January 21 to 26, Dr. Crane was assisted in several medicolegal investigations by two PHR consultants--Clyde Collins Snow, Ph.D., a forensic anthropologist from Norman, Oklahoma, and Margarita Arruza, M.D., a forensic pathologist from Jacksonville, Florida. Dr. Snow returned to Chiapas from February 23 to 26 to examine the skeletal remains of three men allegedly executed by army soldiers. PHR Executive Director Eric Stover visited Chiapas from March 26 to April 5.

During our visits, we met with victims of human rights abuses and their relatives; forensic specialists in Mexico City and Chiapas; prisoners; experts on indigenous affairs; church workers; journalists; government officials, including staff members of the National Commission of Human Rights; and representatives of nongovernmental human rights groups. On several occasions, our representatives observed or participated in forensic investigations, including autopsies and the examination of skeletal remains. We also interviewed witnesses and reviewed postmortem and crime scene photographs (see Chapter VI and Appendix A).

In the final chapter of this report, PHR and HRW/Americas conclude that the CNDH, the federal and state Attorneys General offices, and the military Judicial Prosecutor's office have failed to investigate the violations of human rights and international humanitarian law described in this report in an impartial, thorough, and timely manner. Our organizations believe those responsible for past abuses should be held accountable, both because we feel a duty to the victims and their families and because we believe that such accountability provides the most secure foundation for future respect for human rights and humanitarian law.

In this report, Physicians for Human Rights and Human Rights Watch/Americas recommend the following measures:

• We call on the EZLN to enforce discipline within its ranks in conformity with the Geneva Conventions, which the EZLN leadership has pledged to respect. The EZLN should make public the disciplinary measures taken against its members who have violated international humanitarian law.

• The EZLN officers have the responsibility of instructing their soldiers in the rules of war, especially in Common Article 3 of the Geneva Conventions of 1949 and Protocol II, which describe the rights of the wounded and sick to receive medical care in time of noninternational armed conflict. EZLN officers should also inform those under their command that they will be disciplined for any infringements of international humanitarian law.

• The Mexican government should ensure that any acts by either government or EZLN forces which constitute violations of human rights or humanitarian law are fully and independently investigated and that those responsible for such violations are identified and prosecuted in civilian courts. The Mexican government should clarify the amnesty law enacted to ensure that it is not applied to exempt those persons from criminal prosecution or conviction. Moreover, officials with chain-of-command responsibility who ordered or tolerated criminal acts, especially torture, rape, and extrajudicial executions, should be held criminally responsible for those acts.

• The Congress or judiciary should investigate the circumstances in which Mexican armed forces were authorized to disregard and infringe due process and constitutional rights and guarantees during the Chiapas conflict. This investigation should examine the chain-of-command structure to determine what level such authorization was given. In the future, the government should ensure observance of constitutional constraints on the participation of the armed forces in law enforcement activities such as the detention and questioning of suspects, and ensure that due process guarantees are respected at all times.

• Based on the anthropological and preliminary genetic findings of its forensic experts, PHR and HRW/Americas conclude that *prima facie* evidence exists (see Appendix A and B) to charge Mexican army personnel in the detention, torture, and murder of three men last seen in army custody in the ejido of Morelia on January 7, 1994. As a first step, the Mexican government should arrest immediately the army officers who had command responsibility for the counterinsurgency operation in Morelia. Officials suspected of responsibility for these killings should also be suspended from active duty during the investigation.

• HRW/Americas and PHR believe the PGR has attempted to cover up possible military involvement in the summary executions of five men in the Ocosingo marketplace on January 3 (see Chapter VI). When confronted with contradictions in their findings, including the misidentification of one of the bodies, the PGR failed to reconsider their exoneration of military personnel as possible suspects in these murders. The Mexican government should appoint immediately an independent, special commission of inquiry to investigate the five killings in Ocosingo and the assault on the minibus (see Chapter VI).

• We call on the National Commission of Human Rights (CNDH) to release its findings and recommendations in a timely manner, even if they contradict conclusions drawn by other agencies, governmental or otherwise.

II. THE NEW YEAR'S DAY REBELLION

Shortly after midnight on New Year's Day of 1994, hundreds of Indian peasants, armed with machetes and rifles and belonging to a hitherto-unknown rebel force, the Zapatista National Liberation Army (*Ejército Zapatista de Liberación Nacional/EZLN*), took over the county seats of San Cristóbal de las Casas, Ocosingo, Altamirano, and Las Margaritas in the state of Chiapas. In San Cristóbal, a popular tourist center, the rebels broke into the city hall, ransacked public records, torched the building that housed the state Attorney General's office, and looted stores. Townspeople and numerous tourists looked on in amazement, but were not attacked or molested. Similar scenes occurred in the other occupied towns.

As the day wore on, the rebels barricaded main roads with tree trunks, cut phone and power lines, and handed out leaflets announcing a "declaration of war" against the Mexican army and the administration of President Carlos Salinas de Gortari. The leaflets said that the rebels were exercising a constitutional right to take up arms as a last resort against "more than seventy years of poverty, injustice, and exploitation," and called on "the other powers of the nation" to restore the rule of law and "depose the dictator."[6] They also urged international organizations and the International Committee of the Red Cross (ICRC) to monitor the conflict and protect civilians. EZLN leaders considered

---

[6] The EZLN identified its members as descendants of Pancho Villa and Emiliano Zapata, heroes of the Mexican revolution of 1910, who "have nothing, absolutely nothing, not a suitable roof, nor land, nor work, nor health, nor adequate food, nor education, nor the right to freely and democratically elect our representatives, nor independence from foreigners, nor justice for ourselves or our children." EZLN letter, entitled "El Despertador," translated from Spanish, to the Mexican people, January 1, 1994.

7

themselves bound by the Geneva Conventions and ordered their combatants to respect the lives of prisoners and the wounded.

Journalists described the rebels as mostly indigenous Mayan Indians, who wore green uniforms and red bandannas tied around their faces. Some of the rebels carried modern assault rifles and pistols; others were armed only with antiquated hunting rifles, and even imitation guns made of wood. Although their numbers remains a matter of conjecture, press reports estimated the total at two thousand, and by all accounts they were well organized and disciplined.

Rebel leaders could be distinguished by their *pasamontañas*, or black ski masks. One of them, an obviously educated man not of Indian descent who identified himself as *Subcomandante* Marcos, held an impromptu press conference from a balcony in the city hall of San Cristóbal de las Casas.[7]

The uprising, Marcos said, had been ten years in preparation and was timed to coincide with the adoption of the North American Free Trade Agreement (NAFTA)--a treaty he characterized as "a death certificate for the Indian peoples of Mexico."

Although the Zapatistas had been known to be in training for years in secret camps near the Lacandón jungle, the offensive caught the state and federal governments off-guard. During 1993, the influential daily *La Jornada* and the political weekly *Proceso* had reported on clandestine guerrilla activities in Chiapas, and extensive army operations against them.[8] However, the federal

---

[7] "Comandante Marcos: el EZLN tiene 10 años de preparación," *La Jornada,* January 2, 1994.

[8] In March 1993, army troops raided homes and arbitrarily arrested villagers in the rural communities of Mitzitón and San Isidro el Ocotal near San Cristóbal de las Casas, after the charred remains of two men

government, presumably with an eye towards the negotiations then underway for Mexico's entry into NAFTA, denied the reports and stated flatly that "there are no guerrillas in Mexico."[9]

The Context of the Conflict

The uprising was the first of a chain of events in 1994 that suggested that Mexico's renowned political stability had been in reality a carefully preserved illusion.[10] The local causes of the rebellion are not hard to find. Chiapas has the worst socioeconomic conditions in Mexico, a long history of agrarian

---

thought to be soldiers were found after they had vanished while on patrol in the area. There were shoot-outs with supposed guerrillas and house-to-house searches two months later in the ejido of Pataté Viejo, near Ocosingo. Human rights abuses committed by Mexican troops during these operations were documented by Amnesty International and by Minnesota Advocates for Human Rights. For a review of evidence of guerrilla activity in 1993, see, for example, Guillermo Correa, "Hay guerrilleros en Chiapas desde hace ocho años, grupos radicales infiltraron a la Iglesia y a las comunidades," *Proceso*, September 20, 1993.

[9] Mexico's Minister of Government (equivalent to the Minister of the Interior), Patrocinio González Garrido--who until January 1993 was governor of Chiapas--was quoted as saying, "There are land invasions, and clashes (that leave) injured and even dead, but that's a far cry from a guerrilla problem....These are internal conflicts, not an insurgency." Andrés Oppenheimer, "Image-conscious Mexico: Guerrillas, What guerrillas?" *Miami Herald*, June 28, 1993. In an interview published in the July 1994 edition of *Vanity Fair*, Marcos claimed that the army had come upon rebel encampments on several occasions in 1993, but held back from launching a full-scale attack which might have ended in a bloodbath.

[10] The others were the assassination on March 23 of Luis Donaldo Colosio, candidate of the ruling Institutional Revolutionary Party *(Partido Revolucionario Institucional,* PRI) in the August 21 elections, a string of kidnappings and ransomings of business magnates and of bomb attacks attributed to drug mafias.

conflict, and a record for injustice and human rights abuse unparalleled anywhere else in the country.

Statistics on rural poverty in Chiapas are grim. Although the state is rich in agricultural resources and livestock, and its hydroelectric schemes generate sixty percent of the nation's electricity, Chiapas is the poorest state in Mexico. It has thirty percent illiteracy (two and one-half times the national average), nearly half its homes lack plumbing, and one-third are without electricity. Population growth during the 1980's was 4.51 percent, more than double the average for the country as a whole. The proportion of children between six and fourteen years of age attending school is 71.3 percent, well below Mexico's average of 85.8 percent. There is one doctor for every 1,500 inhabitants.

Poverty is concentrated among the state's indigenous Mayan inhabitants, thirty-two percent of whom (aged five or older) are monolingual, that is, they speak one of several Indian languages (principally Tzeltal, Tzotzil, Chol, Zoque, and Tojolabal) but no Spanish. The regions affected directly by the conflict score highest on all the poverty indicators mentioned above. More than half the inhabitants of Altamirano (pop. 18,909) aged fifteen or older cannot read or write; forty-eight percent in Las Margaritas (pop. 107,777), and forty-seven percent in Ocosingo (pop. 147,100). Almost a third of Ocosingo's Indian population are monolingual, and two out of five children do not attend school.[11] Only 3,769 have access to social security.

The economy of Chiapas is dominated by agriculture and the exploitation of its natural resources, particularly oil. Rapid population growth and the collapse of earnings from the region's four principal products--timber, cattle, coffee, and corn--have brought intense competition for land and natural resources, and

---

[11] "Las cifras de la miseria: la desnutrición es la principal causa de muerte," *Síntesis,* Suplemento Especial, "Chiapas: La Guerra de los Olvidados," January 1994, p. 3.

have inflamed social tensions. The agrarian reforms which followed the Mexican revolution of 1910 were never fully implemented in Chiapas, and land tenure remains highly skewed in favor of large landowners. In the regions affected by the conflict, particularly Ocosingo and Altamirano, vast cattle ranches were created by violent and illegal invasions of *ejido* (community-owned) land, and the antagonism between the predominantly *mestizo* (mixed race) ranchers and Indian subsistence farmers has been a cause of permanent tensions. Other important factors are political divisions in municipalities and religious conflicts in indigenous communities. These conflicts have aligned a wide array of independent peasant associations and unions on one side against landowners, PRI local authorities (alleged in many cases to have been elected fraudulently), as well as state government officials, on the other. Ranchers and small-holders, generally loyal to the PRI, have thrown their weight behind the authorities.[12]

For years, order has been maintained in Chiapas by an informal alliance of large landowners, cattle ranchers, and lumber barons (most with close ties to the PRI), officials in state and local government, and representatives of the PRI's mass organizations, especially its peasant wing, the National Peasant Confederation (CNC). Local influence-holders, known in Mexico as *caciques*, range from an elite group of landowning families to the owners of village stores and liquor franchises, who sometimes double as elected village or ejido leaders. These groups traditionally deliver the vote for PRI candidates at election time in return for substantial concessions. When threatened by opposition or unrest, they may resort to armed posses and hired guns (*pistoleros*, or *guardias blancas*) to rid themselves of troublesome agitators. The frequent collusion of municipal and state officials has ensured that the perpetrators of abuses are rarely punished. On the contrary, the state or municipal police, as well as many judges and civil

---

[12] Luis Hernández, "The New Mayan War," *NACLA Report on the Americas,* No. 5, 1994.

authorities, often misuse the law in their own favor to repress those who oppose the alliance, particularly Indians. While Indians are detained, tortured, and imprisoned often on trumped-up charges, those responsible for abuses are rarely arrested or charged. All too often, land conflicts are resolved by the use of force and skullduggery.

Despite these long-standing divisions, the PRI has consistently recorded landslide results in federal, state, and municipal elections. In the 1988 presidential election, President Salinas took eighty-five to ninety percent of the vote in Chiapas, one of the highest percentages in Mexico. In a country whose political system has been disfigured for decades by systematic electoral fraud favoring the ruling party, rural states like Chiapas again score the highest.[13] The PRI has never lost a gubernatorial race in Chiapas and currently controls 109 of the state's 110 municipalities.[14]

---

[13] According to Mexico scholar Andrew Reding, "In the 9th Congressional District, which includes Ocosingo and two other towns occupied by the Zapatistas, the PRI received one hundred percent of all votes cast in ten of the district's nineteen municipalities. In fact, when the Zapatistas ransacked the local PRI office, they discovered ballots from a previous election that should have been in the possession of the electoral authorities." Andrew Reding, "Chiapas is Mexico: The Imperative of Political Reform," *World Policy Journal,* March 21, 1994, p. 17. For information on electoral fraud in rural areas, see Alberto Aziz and Juan Molinar, "Los resultados electorales" in Pablo González Casanova, *Segundo Informe sobre la Democracia,* 1990, and The Rosenblüth Foundation, *Geografía de las Elecciones Presidenciales de México, 1988.*

[14] The Zapatista revolt was the catalyst for a wave of take-overs of city halls throughout the state. "As of early February 1994, nine of the state's 111 municipalities had been taken over by local citizens' groups. Residents of twenty-five others had formally requested the removal of their municipal presidents, and Chiapanecos from sixty-two different municipalities had an ongoing protest in the capital of Tuxtla Gutiérrez calling for an audit of local government funds, among other demands."

Since the mid-1980s, national and international human rights organizations have documented violations of human rights and the denial of justice in Chiapas. Violations include the murder by hired guns of rural organizers, lawyers, and journalists; the arbitrary detention and imprisonment on trumped-up charges of peasants involved in land conflicts; widespread torture and ill-treatment; violent land evictions and the destruction and theft of property; and the harassment of advocates of Indian rights, particularly of priests and human rights workers at the Diocese of San Cristóbal de las Casas.[15]

The Twelve-Day War

The Mexican army was caught off-guard by the New Year's Day rebellion. The most intense fighting began on the following day, as army soldiers repelled an attack by EZLN guerrillas on the military garrison of Rancho Nuevo, seven miles from San Cristóbal. The battle lasted most of the day, and the rebels suffered heavy casualties.

In the meantime, the EZLN forces had occupied several smaller towns, including Chanal, Huixtan, Oxchuc, and Guadalupe

---

See Antonio Tovar, "Takeover Fever," Special Report, *Insight,* March 6, 1994.

[15] For a more detailed background on the intimidation of priests and those who defend Indian land claims, see Human Rights Watch, *Mexico, the New Year's Rebellion: Violations of Human Rights and Humanitarian Law During the Armed Revolt in Chiapas,* Vol. VI, No. 3, March 1, 1994, pp. 5-7. For earlier reports which describe human rights violations in Chiapas and other rural states, see Amnesty International, *Mexico: Human Rights in Rural Areas (1986),* "Continuing human rights violations against members of the Tzeltal indigenous community in Chiapas," AI Index AMR 41/05/93; Americas Watch, *Human Rights in Mexico, a Policy of Impunity (1990),* and *Unceasing Abuses: Human Rights in Mexico One Year After the Introduction of Reform,* September 1991.

Tepeyac. In response, the Mexican army moved into the area with air support and set up road blocks to seal off the occupied towns.

As government troops moved into the towns, the Zapatistas quickly withdrew. For the most part, there were only scattered confrontations. In Ocosingo, however, a detachment of rebels had taken refuge in the market and the town cemetery and had to fight their way out. As the battle raged, several civilians were killed in the crossfire.

By nightfall on January 3, the Ministry of Defense announced that the rebels had left all four towns in the Los Altos area.

Over the next four days, Mexican air force planes strafed the wooded hillsides surrounding the hamlets of El Carrizal, San Antonio Los Baños, El Ocotal, and El Corralito, located just to the south of San Cristóbal de las Casas, where the military believed rebels had taken refuge. Initial press reports spoke of the use of bombs during aerial attacks on the region near Altamirano. The Mexican army denied it had used bombs but admitted that it used rockets and had strafed ground targets with helicopter-mounted machine guns. The attacks caused widespread damage to civilian homes. At least one civilian was killed and several seriously injured as a result of indiscriminate aerial attacks.[16]

---

[16] Agustín Guzmán García, aged six, from the hamlet of Nuevo San Carlos, near Altamirano, was killed by a rocket on January 6, while accompanying his father, Agustín Guzmán Lorenzo, his sister Rosa María Guzmán, and Sebastián Hernández Guzmán, a cousin, to get food. The father was seriously injured by shrapnel, and after a long quest for medical attention, was finally transported by the CNDH to Mexico City where he received specialized attention. The family later received compensation from the Support Fund for Compensation of Widows and Orphans in Areas of Conflict (*Fondo de Apoyo para Indemnización de Viudas y Huérfanos en Areas de Conflicto/FAPIAC*) for the loss of their son. Although the CNDH concluded from its autopsy of the boy's body

14

During the first week of January, army troops conducted house-to-house raids in the Los Altos and border regions, ransacking homes, stealing valuables, and making widespread arrests without warrant. In army-occupied towns, residents were advised to stay in their homes. In Ocosingo, many residents who ventured out to buy food and supplies were killed, apparently in cross-fire, and others were arrested by the army. Meanwhile, the air force continued to bombard suspected rebel strongholds from the air.

By January 6, the army had sealed off the entire combat zone. Journalists and human rights monitors were stopped at army roadblocks mounted on the exit routes from San Cristóbal to the neighboring countryside. Soldiers prevented citizens from leaving or returning to their communities, causing anxiety and hardship, including loss of livestock and possessions. Although the army cited the need to protect civilians as the reason for these measures, it was accused of trying to prevent the press from monitoring army activity. Access to the combat zone was only regained on January 12 as a result of pressure by local human rights organizations. The worst human rights violations documented in this report were, in fact, committed during the week in which journalists and human rights workers were barred from the area.[17]

---

that he was killed by aerial fire, no information was made public as to whether the army or air force had investigated the incident.

[17] Journalists, Mexican and foreign, covered the conflict with professionalism and courage. On January 3, *La Jornada* reporters Ismael Romero, Frida Hartz, Fabrizio León, and David Aponte, who were travelling in clearly marked press vehicles from San Cristóbal to Altamirano and Las Margaritas, were caught in heavy gunfire close to the army base at Rancho Nuevo. Romero was hit in the shoulder by three bullets. Another incident involved a group of journalists travelling in a red minibus clearly identified as a press vehicle, who escaped unharmed after the vehicle was strafed by two Mexican army Hercules planes on January 5 near Corralito. Travelling in the minibus were

Until January 12, the Mexican army had responded to the rebellion using conventional military counterinsurgency tactics. Under mounting public pressure, however, President Salinas suddenly and dramatically abandoned this strategy. Appearing on television that day, he announced a unilateral ceasefire, and began to open channels for direct negotiations with EZLN leaders. Had it not been for that timely decision, violations of human rights would surely have occurred on a far greater scale. Although the government was adamant in rejecting the rebels' claim to belligerent status, its decision to debate reforms of national importance with the leaders of a hitherto-unknown military force is unprecedented in recent Latin American history. It surely reflected a widespread feeling among ordinary urban Mexicans--as evidenced by several opinion surveys--that the Zapatistas had public sympathy on their side.

The Interior Ministry first tried to defuse the New Year's Day rebellion by labelling the insurgents "transgressors," and the Indian rebels as unfortunate victims who had been unscrupulously manipulated by "highly educated and trained" professional agitators, some of whom were foreigners.[18] This argument was abandoned when it became clear that the EZLN was composed overwhelmingly of indigenous peasants, and that its aims and style

---

reporters from *Univision*, *Agence France Presse*, and a photographer and reporter from the magazine *Mira*, Jorge Vargas and Elia Baltazar. Also, *La Jornada* reporters Blanche Petrich, Rosa Rojas, and Gaspar Morquecho were fired on by an army helicopter on January 7 while covering a firefight between the Mexican army and the EZLN on the outskirts of San Cristóbal.

[18] The Minister of the Interior said: "It is important to repeat that this is not an indigenous or peasant movement but the actions of a radical group directed by professionals who are deceiving, and indeed forcing or tricking Indians into participating." See *Informe de la Secretaría de Gobernación con Materiales de la Secretaría de la Defensa Nacional y la Procuraduría General de la República* (undated). Similar official statements were quoted in several national newspapers.

had more in common with well-tried methods of peasant direct action than a traditional leftist guerrilla insurgency.

President Salinas reshuffled his cabinet on January 10. He dismissed the Minister of Government, Patrocinio González Garrido, a noted hardliner during his earlier governorship of Chiapas, and replaced him with Jorge Carpizo MacGregor, a former Supreme Court justice and Attorney General, who earlier had served as the first president of the National Commission of Human Rights (CNDH), the government human rights ombudsman.[19]

President Salinas called on his Foreign Minister, Manuel Camacho Solis, who was widely respected in Mexico as a conciliator and a skilled negotiator, to represent the government in negotiations with the rebels. Camacho, who was promised full presidential backing for his peace-making efforts, announced that he would approach the task as a private citizen, not as a government official. One of his first steps was to seek the advice of the Bishop of San Cristóbal de las Casas, Samuel Ruiz.

Bishop Ruiz has been an outspoken defender of Indians and human rights for more than thirty years. He and the priests and catechists of his diocese have been the target of persistent denunciations and threats by state government officials, the army, and private landowners. In fact, only days before Camacho met with him, Bishop Ruiz and the Fray Bartolomé Human Rights Center, which is attached to the diocese, were accused by state government officials of fomenting and aiding the Zapatista rebellion. The federal authorities did nothing to quash these rumors.

---

[19] Under his leadership the CNDH, a governmental body with quasi-independent investigative authority but no prosecutorial powers, grew and produced thorough, credible investigations into sensitive human rights cases.

President Salinas also met with Jorge Madrazo, the new president of the CNDH, personally backing Madrazo's efforts to establish a special role for the organization in monitoring human rights during the conflict. By that time, the CNDH had established offices in San Cristóbal and the state capital, Tuxtla Gutiérrez. The CNDH staff, which included forensic investigators and attorneys, had already begun receiving and investigating allegations, tracing missing persons, and providing humanitarian relief to displaced persons. The CNDH's role over the next several months would be a delicate one, given its dependency on the government and its limited investigative and decision-making powers.[20]

Founded in June 1990, the CNDH's main function has been to receive and investigate complaints of violations of human rights and to make recommendations to the relevant authorities based on its own findings.[21] The CNDH is also responsible for presenting the government's human rights policies at the national and international levels. However, the CNDH has neither broad investigative powers nor the constitutional authority to carry out these tasks effectively.

---

[20] According to Amnesty International, human rights organizations in Mexico "welcomed the creation of the commission [CNDH]. However, they publicly expressed concern that it was not an independent body and that it did not have full investigatory powers. Many believed that the commission's independence and authority, and therefore its effectiveness, would have been greater had its creation been debated and approved by Congress, rather than by presidential decree." See Amnesty International, *Mexico: Torture with Impunity* (London: Amnesty International, 1991), p. 31.

[21] See Héctor Fix-Zamudio, *Justicia Constitutional, Ombudsman, y Derechos Humanos, Mexico,* D.F.: Comisión Nacional de Derechos Humanos, 1993, pp. 149-247.

After the Ceasefire

Following the ceasefire announcement of January 12, the army stated that it would open fire only if attacked or to defend civilians threatened with violence, and began to reduce its presence in the disputed towns and villages. Although it maintained road blocks at access points to towns and villages, journalists were allowed entry to most of the countryside. Many of them visited remote jungle areas under EZLN control to interview Zapatista leaders, and in particular Subcomandante Marcos, whose ski-masked countenance, sophistication, and self-deprecating wit transformed him almost instantly into a cult figure. The EZLN agreed to respect the ceasefire, and apart from isolated incidents, an uneasy peace has prevailed.

On January 20, President Salinas signed an amnesty law which offered freedom from prosecution for federal crimes committed in the conflict between January 1 and January 20, provided that those seeking amnesty laid down their weapons within thirty days. A similar law was passed on January 22 by the Chiapas state legislature for state crimes.

While the ceasefire halted open fighting on the ground, aerial attacks continued. The army raided homes looking for guerrillas and conducted house-to-house searches in ejidos and indigenous communities outside EZLN control. Arbitrary arrests and torture also continued. In several towns, municipal presidents used the presence of soldiers to settle long-standing scores with civic opposition groups.

Although violations of human rights decreased in the second half of January, the ceasefire did little to ease social tensions in the state. Civic opposition groups, emboldened by the Zapatistas' rapid political advances, denounced malpractices by PRI local authorities in scores of municipalities across the state, occupied town-halls, and in at least one town, Teopisco, deposed the mayor by force.[22]

Peasant groups were quick to take advantage of the army's withdrawal and the pending peace talks. They began to squat on thousands of acres of privately owned ranches and farming land to which they had been often seeking legal title unsuccessfully for years. By mid-April, peasants belonging to the State Council of Indian and Peasant Organizations (CEOIC), which is comprised of 280 Chiapas peasant associations and unions, had occupied 342 estates covering 100,000 hectares. On April 14, the state government, cattlemen and landowners signed an agreement with the organization in which the latter agreed not to undertake further occupations, in exchange for negotiations for the purchase of land and the transfer of titles to the current occupiers. However, at least three hundred other properties were taken over by landless peasants between mid-April and the end of June. There were several cases in which ranchers and smallholders returning to their fields to check on livestock were kidnapped by squatters and held prisoner for several days. Some were allegedly made to do forced labor or sign agreements surrendering property. Ranchers accused the squatters of violating the April 14 agreements which included allowing owners free access to their property.[23]

---

[22] From January 15 to April 10, town halls were occupied by protesters in Mapastepec, Huehuetán, Tuzantán, Cacahotán, Coipanala, Chanal, Teopisco, Siltepec, Bellavista, Jaltenango, Pueblo Nuevo Solistahuacán, Pantelho, Villa de las Rosas, Jiquipilas, and Venustiano Carranza. Onécimo Hidalgo Domínguez, "Antecedentes y Desarrollo del Conflicto en Chiapas," CONPAZ, April 15, 1994.

[23] Fredy Martín Pérez, "La OCEZ detuvo a rancheros de Trinitaria," *El Tiempo,* June 10, 1994; Elio Henríquez and José Gil Olmos, "Detienen militantes de la OCEZ a tres parvifundistas en Chiapas," *La Jornada,* June 22, 1994.

In June, the ranchers threatened to resort to direct action to recover their lands unless the authorities stepped in to restore law and order. However, state governor Javier López Moreno, a Salinas appointee who was committed to supporting the "peace process," was reluctant to use force against the squatters, and the long delays in issuing eviction orders, accompanied by continuing land occupations, further incensed the ranchers and smallholders.[24] In the second week of June, more than five thousand peasants held a week-long sit-in on the steps of the government palace in Tuxtla Gutiérrez. This was followed, within days, by a rival protest mounted by 4,000 members of the state's ranchers' and smallholders' organizations. Two women demanding the return of their properties staged a hunger strike, with their mouths covered by gags bearing the words "Let Mexico Speak!"[25]

At the end of June, the state government finally reached a settlement with the ranchers. It agreed to begin evicting immediately those peasants who had illegally occupied lands after April 14, but to continue negotiating the purchase and reassignment of lands occupied before that date, as well as relocating peasants to other sites. It refused, however, to call on the armed forces "under any circumstances" to carry out the evictions. Owners would be compensated at a rate of forty-five

---

[24] Gonzalo López Camacho, president of the Central Region Ranchers' Union (*Unión Ganadera Regional Centro)*, accused the governor of "allowing the people to have a party, overstepping the limits in demonstrations, after having lived under a hard fist." Candelaria Rodríguez: "Rechazan respuesta del gobierno chiapaneco sobre los deslalojos," *La Jornada*, June 27, 1994.

[25] José Gil Olmos and Candelaria Rodríguez, "Ofrece el gobierno de Chiapas iniciar hoy el desalojo de predios," *La Jornada*, June 28, 1994.

pesos per hectare (approximately $15) for income lost as a result of the occupations.[26]

In Chiapas, at least twenty peasants were killed in land-related disputes between January and April 1994.[27] In some of the cases the main suspects were hired guns paid by landowners, or members of the municipal police force. Among those murdered was Mariano Pérez Díaz, a leader of the Emiliano Zapata Peasant Organization (OCEZ) and also a CEOIC coordinator, who was engaged in the peace agreement consultations in Indian communities in Simojóvel. Eight unidentified gunmen shot him dead outside his home in Simojóvel on March 9, and his son, Jorge Pérez Núñez, was seriously wounded.[28] Both men had previously received death threats. The state governor announced that a special prosecutor, to be chosen by CEOIC, would be appointed to investigate the assaults. Relatives of the deceased leader reportedly accused the Simojóvel local council president of paying gunmen to murder him.[29]

Scores of police arrests of CEOIC members and land evictions, many of them, violent were reported during the third week of September in several districts, especially in Trinitaria and Suchiate.

---

[26] José Gil Olmos: "Desalajo a partir del día 5, acordó López Moreno con los ganaderos," *La Jornada,* July 2, 1994.

[27] Onécimo Hidalgo Domínguez: *Antecedentes y desarrollo del Conflicto en Chiapas,* CONPAZ, April 15, 1994.

[28] Amnesty International, Urgent Action, 102/94 AMR 41/05/94 (Mariano Pérez Diaz and Jorge Pérez Núñez).

[29] Betsy Villarreal and Juna de Dios García Davish, "Gobernador de Chiapas reconoce clima de tensión," *Unomásuno*, March 11, 1994.

The Peace Negotiations

On February 21, peace talks began between the EZLN and the President's envoy Manuel Camacho Solís in the cathedral of San Cristóbal de las Casas. Bishop Ruiz was there as an observer. Before the negotiations started, Marcos had enlisted the support of leaders of six opposition parties to push for broad political reforms. As the August 21 elections drew closer, it became clear that a localized peasant uprising had become the catalyst for a nationwide movement for political and democratic reform. A Market Opinion Research International (a Mexico City survey organization) poll in February showed that support for the uprising had increased from sixty-one percent to seventy-five percent of residents of Mexico City.[30]

On March 2, after protracted disagreement over the scope of the agenda, Camacho and the EZLN negotiators reached a thirty-two point "tentative" agreement on reform measures, and the EZLN delegates said that they would return to their communities to explain the proposals, and that the communities themselves would vote on whether or not to accept them. The proposals included limited autonomy for indigenous communities, a law forbidding discrimination against Indians, and major investment in social services. They also called for breaking up and redistributing land held by privately-owned ranches and redrawing electoral boundaries to permit more Indian representation. The EZLN was skeptical that these measures, although radical on paper, would ever be implemented without national political reforms. The government, however, insisted that such reforms, including guarantees for fair elections, must be negotiated with the political parties and debated in a special session of Congress.

---

[30] Tim Golden, "Rebels Battle for the Hearts of Mexicans," *New York Times*, February 26, 1994.

Immediate prospects for peace received a severe blow when Luis Donaldo Colosio, the PRI's presidential candidate and Salinas' likely successor, was assassinated on March 23 while campaigning in Tijuana. The EZLN promptly declared itself in a state of alert and suspended consultations on the peace measures. Marcos said Colosio's murder was part of a plot within the government to overturn the PRI's reformist current and that a major military offensive against the rebels was in preparation. The EZLN contested government claims that troops were being moved out of the area for "rest and recreation," believing them to have been simply redeployed to areas outside the scrutiny of the media.

On June 10, after more than two months had passed, the "Clandestine Revolutionary Indian Committee" (CCRI), the EZLN's decision-making body, finally announced that it had rejected the government's peace terms. Ninety-eight percent of the communities under EZLN influence had voted against accepting the terms, according to rebel spokesman Subcomandante Marcos. While announcing the end of the dialogue, the EZLN ordered its forces to continue to respect the ceasefire and not to engage in hostilities unless attacked. It also promised not to obstruct the August 21 presidential and congressional elections in territories under its control and to allow polling booths to be installed "under the vigilance of nongovernmental organizations and the International Committee of the Red Cross."[31]

The failure of the San Cristóbal negotiations appears to have been due in large part to the gulf noted earlier between the EZLN's and the government's positions on political reform.[32]

---

[31] Communicado del Comité Clandestino Revolucionario Indígena-Comandancia General del Ejército Zapatista de Liberación Nacional, Mexico, June 10 1994.

[32] On June 16, Jorge Camacho resigned as peace commissioner after being publicly criticized by PRI presidential candidate Ernesto Zedillo, who stated in an interview "We are experiencing a great disillusionment. We were sure that the negotiations had been a success and now the truth

In short, the political and electoral reforms negotiated by the minister of government, Jorge Carpizo, with the opposition parties proved insufficient to convince the EZLN that the PRI was really willing to submit itself to a popular verdict on August 21. On January 27, Jorge Carpizo, the newly-appointed minister of government, had co-signed an "Agreement for Peace, Democracy and Justice" between the PRI and seven opposition parties. From February through July extensive electoral reforms were carried out. They included allowing greater nonpartisan representation on the Federal Electoral Institute (IFE), which designs and oversees the electoral process, the compilation of a new electoral roll subject to external audit, lower limits on campaign spending, greater access of opposition parties to the media, and a package of polling-day anti-fraud measures. However, there was opposition to the reforms both from groups within the PRI's own ranks, who believed they went too far, and from the center-left opposition Democratic Revolutionary Party (*Partido de la Revolución Democratica*--PRD), which criticized them as insufficient.[33] In

---

is that they were a failure." Camacho rejected Zedillo's criticism. In a press conference on the night of his resignation, he said: "For [Zedillo] the central problem is that the list of petitions was answered and the answer was rejected. As a result, the process of negotiation failed. For me, the central problem was to halt the violence, protect the prestige of the Mexican army and shift the agenda from the resignation of the Executive to making new responses to just demands and democratic advances." In his resignation letter addressed to President Salinas, Camacho accused the PRI of censuring his efforts for peace and closing off the possibility of genuine political dialogue. See Rafael Rodríguez Castañeda, "Atrás de las declaraciones de Zedillo, la línea de intolerancia que está dominado en el PRI: Manuel Camacho," *Proceso* No.920, June 20, 1994. On June 23, Camacho was replaced as peace commissioner by the former President of the CNDH, Jorge Madrazo Cuellar.

[33] See Human Rights Watch/Americas' report, *Mexico at the Crossroads, Political Rights and the 1994 Presidential and Congressional Elections*, Vol. VI, Number 9, August 15, 1994, for a detailed analysis of the reforms and their shortcomings.

its communiqué ending the San Cristóbal dialogue, the EZLN categorically rejected the measures.[34]

Retaining its weapons and war footing, the EZLN now threw its weight behind new efforts to forge a nationwide citizens' movement for fundamental political change. Once more it called for President Salinas's resignation, the formation of a transitional government, and the holding of fair and free elections under the supervision of nonpartisan groups. It promised to hold a "national dialogue of all the progressive forces with the central theme of democracy, liberty and, justice for all Mexicans." This so called National Democratic Convention was held during the second week of August on Zapatista-controlled territory. The meeting took place in an enormous timber amphitheater hewn by axe and machete from the Lancandón rainforest. Almost 6,000 delegates, representing hundreds of civil organizations from across the country, attended the convention. They pledged to defeat the PRI in the polls and to organize large-scale civil resistance in the case of fraud.[35]

---

[34] It stated: "The electoral reforms were manifestly inadequate. The maintenance of a vitiated electoral register permits electronic fraud and repeats the usurpation of the popular will." *Comunicado del Comité Clandestino Revolucionario Indígena.*

[35] Ernesto Zedillo, the PRI candidate, won the presidency with 48.77 percent of the vote; the conservative-democratic *Partido de Acción Nacional* took second place, with 25.69 percent for its candidate, Diego Fernández, while PRD candidate Cuauhtémoc Cárdenas came in third, with 17.08 percent. The PRD was alone in contesting the result as fraudulent.

III. THE TOLL OF THE CONFLICT

Officially, more than 145 people are known to have died in the fighting between January 1 and January 12. However, the true death toll is likely to exceed 200. According to unpublished lists made available to HRW/Americas in February by the CNDH, seventy victims had been identified: thirty-eight members of the state police force (*Seguridad Pública del Estado*);[36] thirteen soldiers of the Mexican army; and nineteen civilians. In addition, CNDH records include details of seventy-two unidentified bodies, forty-eight of them interred in unmarked crypts in the San Marcos cemetery of Tuxtla Gutiérrez.

By February, there were reports of additional civilian casualties not recorded in the CNDH's list because the bodies were buried without official authorization or certification of death in the backyards of private homes. In addition, a review of articles filed by Mexican reporters reveals names of civilians killed in crossfire who were not on the CNDH list. Other human remains and fragments have been photographed, but identification was virtually impossible due to their condition.[37]

---

[36] According to a January 2 press bulletin issued by the Ministry of Government, twenty-four of the police casualties were killed on January 1 while resisting the takeover of public buildings by the EZLN when they stormed Ocosingo, Altamirano, Las Margaritas, Abasolo and Chanal. In Altamirano, according to the state Attorney General's office, seven policemen were killed during the Zapatista takeover of the town; in Las Margaritas three were killed defending the city hall; seven police were shot dead in Ocosingo. Seven police, including the chief of the municipal police, were killed in Chanal. Virtually no information has been made public, either by government agencies or nongovernmental groups, about the specific circumstances in which the police died.

[37] Photographs in HRW's possession taken by Carlos Peña Rojas, correspondent for the *Mañana de Reynoso*, show human remains, virtually reduced to bones by scavengers, which were found in various

The number of EZLN combatants killed is unknown; some of them may be interred in the San Marcos Cemetery. There were unconfirmed reports that the army clandestinely cremated more than twenty bodies in a granary in Altamirano.[38] For the most part, the EZLN took care of their dead themselves; they also removed some of their wounded from hospitals. Forty EZLN combatants still remain unaccounted for, according to Subcomandante Marcos in an interview with local human rights workers in March. He said their relatives were urgently seeking information about them, fearing that they might be in detention.

Displacement of the Civilian Population

During the rebellion, thousands of Indian villagers living in conflict zones fled their homes and made their way to camps for displaced persons in the main towns. In February, the Mexican Red Cross estimated there were 35,000 displaced peoples, of whom 18,232 were in camps and the remainder in private homes or homeless. The Ministry of Defense, however, estimated only 20,482 displaced people.[39] Of the thirteen camps set up by state, private, and church agencies, the largest were in Las Margaritas, with more than 7,000 displaced peoples temporarily housed there. Conditions in some of the camps, such as San Cristóbal de las Casas, were reportedly reasonably good, but in others there was said to be severe overcrowding, food shortages, and disease.

---

sites, one apparently a victim of an aerial attack in El Corralito. The decomposed remains of three unknown victims were recovered by the PGR from the community of Corazón de María on January 14. Elio Henríquez, "Surgen en todos partes muertos no-oficiales," *La Jornada,* January 16, 1994.

[38] Juan Manuel Venegas and Oscar Camacho Guzmán, "Informan de fosa común y una bodega con cuerpos calcinados," *La Jornada,* January 16, 1994.

[39] Víctor Ballinas,"Se han desplazado de sus comunidades 35 mil chiapanecos," *La Jornada*, February 11, 1994.

The Mexican army did not engage in a policy of forcible relocation of residents in areas of high EZLN activity. However, there were isolated reports of this practice. According to one report, on January 1, the army entered the community of San Antonio, Ocosingo, where the EZLN had been the night before. Villagers were told that they were being evacuated on the pretext that there was no electricity, and for their protection. The women were taken in three vehicles to Palenque and Villahermosa. Male villagers were taken to Ocosingo, where they were interrogated all night with their hands behind their neck. The next day they were released and ordered to join their relatives. They walked without money or food towards Palenque for about 90 miles and then a vehicle picked them up and took them the rest of the way.[40]

In providing emergency aid to civilians, the Mexican army discriminated against those women who were not able to produce their husbands when they asked for assistance. These women, or their husbands, were considered suspects, and they were denied food. This practice, which was widely reported in the press and denounced by nongovernmental human rights groups, was a deplorable misuse of humanitarian aid for military objectives. On January 11, Francisco Gómez Santiz's wife waited in line in Altamirano to receive food rations from the army. She was told she must present her husband to receive food. When he arrived, military personnel detained him. Mr. Gómez was trussed up, blindfolded, and flown by helicopter to what he took to be a military base, where he allegedly was beaten and tortured with electric shocks. He was released in Tuxtla Gutiérrez on January 15.[41]

---

[40] Coordinación de los Organismos No-Gubernamentales de San Cristóbal de las Casas Por la Paz (CONPAZ), *Bulletin No. 16, San Antonio, Municipality of Ocosingo,* January 20, 1994.

[41] Informe preliminar de la Comisión Mexicana de Defensa y Promoción de los Derechos Humanos, El Centro de Derechos Humanos Miguel Agustin Pro-Juarez A.C., El Centro de Derechos Humanos Fray Francisco de Vitoria, A.C., y Red Nacional de Organismos Civiles de

Numerous press reports suggest that EZLN intimidation was a cause of displacement. Many of those interviewed in the camps said they left their land, animals, and crops because of EZLN threats. Thus, Melesio Pérez Méndez of Altamirano, who arrived at a refuge in Las Margaritas with his wife and seven children, complained that the guerrillas "threatened us, forcing us to join them or abandon our land ... we had to leave without bringing anything with us, just the clothes we were wearing."[42]

Israel López Aguilar, a refugee from San Isidro village, said he fled with his family to the government-held town of Las Margaritas after repeated harassment from Zapatistas trying to recruit him. "They had weapons. They wanted us to join them, but we didn't want to, so we left," he said. In Las Margaritas, government relief workers greeted his family with a sack of food and kept the supplies flowing. After several weeks, López said his family tried to return home with their food and supplies, only to see them confiscated on arrival by the rebels. López said he returned to Las Margaritas and has remained there ever since.[43]

Theft, vandalism, and cattle-rustling were also widely denounced. Ranchers' protests of these alleged crimes mounted during February, and were echoed in several Ministry of Defense bulletins alleging the involvement of unidentified armed men believed to be Zapatistas. In February, the PGR announced that it was carrying out a major investigation of the incidents. It stated:

Derechos Humanos "Todos los Derechos Para Todos." (Report to the Inter-American Commission on Human Rights, 85th Session, February 10, 1994). (Hereafter referred to as *Informe Preliminar*).

[42] Salvador Guerrero Chiprés, "Llegan a Altamirano 50 indígenas más, desplazados por el EZLN," *La Jornada*, February 17, 1994, p.8.

[43] Todd Robberson, "Mexico Takes the Initiative from Rebels," *Washington Post*, July 6, 1994.

According to reports received, the inhabitants of various indigenous communities of Los Altos de Chiapas are facing a desperate situation which has forced them to move to safer locations, in order to avoid the abuses committed by the EZLN in areas under its control.[44]

Responsibility for these incidents was rarely clear-cut. Indian villagers from the Saltillo ejido in Las Margaritas charged that ranchers had carried out attacks dressed as Zapatistas in order to incite the population against the rebels.[45] Deliberate rumor-mongering was another factor. In some divided municipalities, the authorities accused their political opponents of being Zapatistas, taking advantage of the conflict to abduct them and hand them over to the army. There were also credible allegations that the mayors of Las Margaritas and Altamirano, in collusion with ranchers and caciques, had bused anti-EZLN peasants into town, where they formed a volatile and intimidating mob, threatening and harassing those on humanitarian missions.[46]

Particularly disturbing was the hate-campaign conducted by the mayor and the ranchers against the Vincentian nuns who run the San Carlos Hospital in Altamirano (see Chapter VII). This facility had provided medical assistance impartially to both sides during the fighting. During the last week of February, the hospital was besieged by angry crowds. CNDH officials were

---

[44] "Inició la PGR investigación sobre despojos en Chiapas," *La Jornada*, February 13, 1994, p.10.

[45] Elio Henríquez, Ricardo Alemán, and Víctor Ballinas, "Campesinos de la CNPI ocupan 18 fincas 'abandonadas' en Chiapas," *La Jornada*, February 15, 1994, p.5.

[46] Víctor Ballinas,"Piden en un mítin destituir al alcalde de las Margaritas," *La Jornada*, February 12, 1994, p.5.

present from February 20-24 to help prevent violence, and later called on the state governor to open a criminal investigation into the threats and to give the nuns police protection.[47]

[47] Roberto Garduño, "Hallazgo de cuerpos y amenazas contra monjas en Altamirano," *La Jornada*, February 12, 1994.

IV. VIOLATIONS OF THE LAWS OF WAR BY THE EZLN

The EZLN acknowledged itself to be bound by the Geneva Conventions of 1949, and called on international organizations and the International Committee of the Red Cross (ICRC) to monitor the conflict. The EZLN also demanded that the government recognize the rebel army as a belligerent force (which it refused to do) and continued to press this demand during the peace negotiations in February. Regardless of the legal status of the conflict or of the adversaries, both parties were obliged to respect the basic humanitarian principles set forth in Article 3 Common to the Geneva Conventions of 1949.[48]

---

[48] Common Article 3 provides: "In the case of armed conflict not of an international character occurring in the territory of one of the High Contracting Parties, each Party to the conflict shall be bound to apply, as a minimum, the following provisions:

(1) Persons taking no active part in the hostilities, including members of armed forces who have laid down their arms and those placed *hors de combat* by sickness, wounds, detention, or any other cause, shall in circumstances be treated humanely, without any adverse distinction founded on race, colour, religion or faith, sex, birth or wealth, or any other similar criteria. To this end the following acts are and shall remain prohibited at any time and in any place whatsoever with respect to the above-mentioned persons:

    (a) violence to life and person, in particular murder of all kinds, mutilation, cruel treatment and torture;

    (b) taking of hostages;

    (c) outrages upon personal dignity, in particular humiliating and degrading treatment;

    (d) in passing of sentences and the carrying out of executions without previous judgement pronounced by a regularly constituted court, affording all the judicial guarantees which are recognized as indispensable by civilized peoples;

(2) The wounded and sick shall be collected and cared for.

An international humanitarian body, such as the International

HRW/Americas' concerns regarding violations of the laws of war by the rebel forces were set out in an earlier report on the conflict.[49] Since then, HRW/Americas and PHR have obtained the transcript of an interview with Subcomandante Marcos, conducted in March by a human rights investigator, which gives the EZLN leader's reactions to human rights criticism. In its earlier report, HRW/Americas concluded that the EZLN had violated Common Article 3 by taking hostages. While occupying Ocosingo on January 2, the EZLN took four men hostage, all of them members of a ranching family. One of them, Dr. Francisco Talango, the town ophthalmologist, was shot dead after he had been released or escaped. The EZLN has not accepted responsibility for the death of Talango. However, in the interview, Marcos said that the EZLN was conducting an investigation into the conduct of its troops in Ocosingo.

There were other reports of civilians who were shot and killed by Zapatista troops, while held captive or seeking to escape. Thus, during the occupation by the EZLN of the town of Chanal from January 1 to January 6, a teacher, Ricardo Gómez López, who tried to escape on board a minibus--presumably after refusing to hand it over to the guerrillas--was shot and killed. He is

---

Committee of the Red Cross, may offer its services to the parties to the conflict.

The Parties to the conflict should endeavor to bring into force, by means of special agreements, all or part of the other provisions of the present Convention.

The application of the preceding provisions shall not affect the legal status of the parties to Parties to the conflict.

[49] Human Rights Watch/Americas, *Mexico, the New Year's Rebellion: Violations of Human Rights and Humanitarian Law During the Armed Revolt in Chiapas,* Vol. VI, No. 3, March 1, 1994, pp. 13-16.

reported to have died after the rebels refused to allow him to be taken to hospital.[50]

On January 20, Luciano Jiménez was reportedly killed by rebels at an EZLN roadblock on the road to Pichucalco. According to testimonies collected by the CNDH, Jiménez was challenged by rebel soldiers when he announced that he was on his way to a political meeting. He was allegedly shot dead when he tried to pass the cordon. His body was buried by the EZLN but could not be found subsequently. Jiménez's brother, Jacinto, was held overnight as a prisoner, and after his release allegedly was closely watched to make sure he told no one of the incident.[51]

Both the PGR and the CNDH allege that the EZLN also abducted civilians in Oxchuc on the same day as the Ocosingo kidnappings. Pablo Santiz Gómez, an Oxhuc bus driver, was visited by a group of some thirty Zapatistas who commandeered his bus in the early morning, taking him and his son Uber with them. Representatives of HRW/Americas interviewed their relatives in February and May but have been unable to determine whether force or threats were, in fact, used. The bullet-riddled vehicle was later found abandoned near the army base at Rancho Nuevo, where a fierce battle had taken place. Two of the fourteen bodies found lying close to the bus were identified as those of the abducted civilians.[52] Oxchuc civilians Fernando Santíz Gómez, the assistant town councillor, and 20-year-old César Méndez

---

[50]Elio Henríquez, Ricardo Alemán, and David Aponte, "Chanal, uno de los últimos reductos en poder del EZLN," *La Jornada,"* January 7, 1994, p. 5. This report confirms a bulletin issued by the Ministry of Defense on events on Chanal, which refers to the assassination of a teacher who refused to cooperate with the EZLN. SEDENA Bulletin, No. 9, January 7, 1994.

[51] Matilde Pérez, "Culpan al EZLN de un asesinato y un secuestro en el camino a Pichucalco," *La Jornada*, February 17, 1994, p. 6.

[52] This case is discussed further in Chapter V.

Gómez were also among those whose bodies were recovered and identified. The municipal authorities claimed that all four men were abducted by the EZLN. Marcos, however, denies that any civilians were abducted in Oxchuc, and insists that no civilians were present on the bus.[53]

On that same day, January 2, EZLN forces kidnapped Absalón Castellanos Domínguez, a former Chiapas governor and army general, from his ranch near Las Margaritas. Castellanos, aged seventy, was held for forty-five days, much of the time blindfolded, and taken to the EZLN's remote hideout in Guadelupe Tepeyac. On February 16, as a token of faith on the eve of the peace conference, he was released to an ICRC representative in a televised ceremony attended by Bishop Ruiz, Manuel Camacho, and the press. Earlier the EZLN had declared its intention to "bring to justice" Castellanos, accusing him of illegally acquiring land and personal riches, and of murdering three peasant leaders. Before he was released, the former governor was made to listen to a detailed summary of the accusations. Castellanos told reporters that he had been well treated and, according to press reports, the ICRC certified him to be in good health.

Marcos has claimed that Castellanos was still on active service, and as such was a legitimate prisoner of war. Our information is that the former governor was retired from military service, and exercised no military command in the Chiapas conflict. Furthermore, as a former state governor and symbol of the Chiapas landowning/governing class, Castellanos' capture was an obvious publicity coup, rather than a military action. PHR and

---

[53] In the interview mentioned above, Marcos claimed that the EZLN commandeered a bus in Altamirano, and that it was used to transport a rebel "assault unit" to attack the state prison outside San Cristóbal de las Casas. The bus then drove to Rancho Nuevo "to see what was happening there," and was attacked. He also admitted that a bus was "taken" in Oxchuc, but insisted that there were no civilians aboard.

HRW/Americas considers this kidnapping to have been indefensible under the laws of war.

In addition to hostage-taking, there are reports that the EZLN used threats or harassment to gain adherents. However, the EZLN does not appear to have used force systematically. There is evidence, based on a press interview with a captured rebel, that he had been forced to join the EZLN under threat of losing his land. It was also reported that some prisoners accused of being Zapatistas said in their defense that they had been "tricked" into joining the rebels. However, the circumstances of their recruitment by the EZLN were unclear; there were reports in several locations of Indians who went along with the rebels on the spur of the moment.

HRW/Americas and PHR were concerned also by eyewitness reports which suggest that EZLN combatants shielded themselves by mingling with civilians during the battle in Ocosingo, thereby endangering the lives of civilians. In the interview mentioned above Marcos strongly disputed these accounts. He asserted that the EZLN had sought wherever possible to avoid fighting in crowded urban areas, and that Ocosingo had been the exception because the army succeeded in pinning down the rebels before they could leave town, forcing them to fight their way out.[54] The eyewitness reports do not offer a firm conclusion as to whether the Zapatistas had used civilians deliberately, or whether the civilians were sympathizers who chose to stay with the Zapatistas despite personal risk. It should be noted, however, that "neither shielding nor the

---

[54] According to Marcos, "What happened was that when we entered the towns many people got enthusiastic and joined our ranks, because everyone was excited and all that, but strictly speaking all those who wanted to fight were uniformed. That is one of the rules of war of the Geneva Conventions. We did not take any civilians, not even people dressed in civilian clothes. Everyone had their uniform and position in the military structure under the corresponding superior officer."

37

voluntary presence of civilians at a military target operate to relieve the other side of its obligation to minimize harm to civilians."[55]

After the EZLN returned to its base in Guadelupe Tepeyac, it imposed a "war tax" on outsiders entering the area under its control. The tax, exacted at gunpoint, hindered movement in and out of the area because drivers were unwilling to pay, and thus affected the supply of food and other basic necessities. The rebels lifted the tax on February 17 as one of the concessions made immediately before peace negotiations began. It was later re-imposed, and has been explicitly acknowledged and defended by EZLN leaders.[56]

---

[55] Although not legally applicable to the Chiapas conflict, The Second Protocol to the Geneva Conventions of 1949 provides a relevant standard. Article 13 states that:
1. The civilian population and individual civilians shall enjoy general protection against the dangers arising from military operations. To give effect to this protection, the following rules shall be observed in all circumstances.

2. The civilian population as such, as well as individual civilians, shall not be the object of attack. Acts or threats of violence, the primary purpose of which is to spread terror among the civilian population, are prohibited.

3. Civilians shall enjoy the protection afforded by this Part, unless and for such time as they take a direct part in hostilities."

[56] Marcos, nevertheless, has pointed out that the EZLN has strict rules regarding the tax and punishes infringements as robbery. "If a rancher has to pay twenty percent of his possessions as a war tax and they take everything he has, that is robbery according to our laws, or if a farm does not exceed the fifty hectares established by our laws as a limit and is invaded, that is robbery too." Furthermore, only community representatives are authorized to exact taxes, and combatants do not have this authority. Marcos admitted, however, that violations of the EZLN laws were "very probable," especially in the jungle zone. Interview by local human rights workers with Subcomandante Marcos, March 1994.

V. VIOLATIONS OF HUMAN RIGHTS AND HUMANITARIAN LAW BY THE MEXICAN ARMY

On the basis of our research, and that of other national and international nongovernmental human rights organizations, PHR and HRW/Americas believe that the Mexican army was responsible for serious violations of human rights and humanitarian law during the fighting and in its aftermath. The abuses, which are described here and in the next chapter, include

- summary executions of wounded or captured combatants, and of civilians in detention;

- widespread arbitrary arrest, prolonged incommunicado detention, and torture;

- indiscriminate attacks on civilian targets; and

- violations of medical neutrality.

Most of these abuses took place during the fighting in early January and received considerable coverage in the national and international press. By the end of that month, systematic human rights violations by the army had virtually ceased as the government prepared to open a dialogue with the insurgents. However, isolated incidents continued to be reported from February through June 1994. Most of them occurred at army roadblocks controlling access to and from EZLN-occupied territory. In general, they consisted of harassment and intimidation of people entering or leaving the zone who were suspected of helping or sympathizing with the insurgents.

On March 19, for instance, a truck carrying food to the San Carlos Hospital was stopped at a roadblock in Altamirano; the soldiers claimed that the food was "aid for the Zapatistas" (the Zapatistas had sympathizers but no combatants in Altamirano). On April 29, Rebeca Collazo López, from the community of

Betania, Teopisco municipality, was wounded when the army fired on a minibus at the Rancho Nuevo roadblock outside San Cristóbal de las Casas. At 8:45 am on May 5, Marisa Kramsky Espinoza, a photographer, was arbitrarily detained for more than an hour at a roadblock between Toniná and Ocosingo when returning from a visit to EZLN occupied territory. She was forced to look at a collection of gruesome photographs of victims of the fighting in Ocosingo, on the pretext that she might help identify some of the victims.

On June 21 at 4:30 pm, two apparently drunken soldiers hammered on the door of Samuel Sánchez Morales' house in Altamirano. The soldiers allegedly pulled him out of bed (he was resting after returning home from work), beat him, and threatened to kill him and members of his family, accusing them of being Zapatistas. On June 4, three Tzeltal women were allegedly tortured and raped after being detained at an army road block at Altamirano.

After allegations of army abuses in early January became widely known, the Ministry of National Defense established offices in major towns to receive citizens' complaints, and promised that all such complaints would be thoroughly investigated. The Ministry has since roundly denied that its troops committed any human rights violations. For instance, in reply to a report by the National Network of Nongovernmental Human Rights Organizations/"All Rights For All," which had documented 127 complaints against soldiers, the Ministry replied that its office for citizens' complaints had "investigated and was able to resolve all of them, without finding any responsibility on the part of military personnel."[57] However, no details were provided about the scope, methods, and conclusions of these investigations.

---

[57] "SEDENA Rejects Chiapas Human Rights Charges," *La Jornada,* April 21, 1994. (English translation from FBIS-LAT-94-079, April 25, 1994).

Arbitrary Arrest and Detention

Despite the intensity of the fighting in the first week, the Mexican government did not introduce a state of emergency, even one restricted to the actual combat zones. Although constitutional guarantees were not suspended or limited in any way, the Mexican army appeared to act as if it had assumed *de facto* state of emergency powers. It detained, interrogated, and transported suspects without legal warrant, refused civilian access to villages and communities, buried bodies without civil procedures, and carried out its own autopsy examinations of civilian victims, thereby undermining the authority of responsible civilian officials. These infringements of due process had no basis in law, but to our knowledge no court has deemed them illegal or unconstitutional.

In the past, constitutional protection from arbitrary arrest has counted for little in Chiapas, even under "normal" conditions. One incident can serve as an example. On May 24, 1993, more than six months before the uprising, eight residents of Pataté Viejo, near Ocosingo, were detained when hundreds of soldiers, searching for guerrillas, entered the town. According to eyewitnesses, the troops assembled the entire village of over one hundred people on the basketball court, searched every home and then detained the eight after allegedly finding weapons in their homes. A delegation from Minnesota Advocates for Human Rights (MAHR), which visited Pataté Viejo on the following day, reported that none of the detainees' wives had been informed of their husbands' whereabouts. Official reasons given for the arrests varied widely, with the army, the PGR, and the Ministry of Defense giving entirely different versions; they agreed only that the incident did not involve a breach of the law. MAHR concluded that "the military conducted a sweep of the Pataté community, apparently looking for illegal weapons or whatever else they could find. The soldiers did not have arrest warrants, and they did not appear to be looking for specific individuals at the time."[58]

---

[58]Minnesota Advocates for Human Rights, *Civilians at Risk: Military and Police Abuses in the Mexican Countryside,* August 1993, pp. 18-22.

Such practices have been common for years in Chiapas, although other groups, such as the state security police, the federal and state judicial police, and even civilian gunmen have largely been responsible.[59] Despite the efforts of local and national human rights organizations, and a handful of newspapers to publicize the abuses, they have attracted little attention abroad or in Mexico. The concerted army raids in January brought them to public notice for the first time. According to the National Network of Nongovernmental Human Rights Organizations "All Rights for All," 133 people were arbitrarily arrested (i.e., without legal warrant) in January 1994, of whom 108 were released and twenty-five were subsequently located in the Cerro Hueco penitentiary, outside Tuxtla Gutiérrez.[60]

Army conduct during its pursuit of the EZLN and Zapatista sympathizers in early January was similar to earlier military operations described in the MAHR report. The army swept into villages or communities, systematically ransacking homes and often assembling at gunpoint the male population in the main public area (often, in a Mexican village, a basketball court). Peasants were then singled out (sometimes by a civilian authority, an informer, or from a list of names carried by the soldiers) during a drawn-out field "investigation." The soldiers would interrogate villagers, sometimes accompanied by beatings and torture, and ransack homes, stores and churches, ostensibly looking for weapons. Theft and destruction of property was widespread. There were no warrants for arrest; their legal grounds were determined several days later, i.e., after detainees had been handed over to the Public Ministry (the state or federal Attorney General's office) and remanded in custody. By then, the detainees had made "declarations" without the presence of a lawyer, and the proceedings were conducted in Spanish, which many Tzeltal and Tzotzil Indians can understand only with

---

[59] See Americas Watch, *Human Rights in Mexico: a Policy of Impunity,* June 1990, pp. 37-41, for a description of abuses in the Mexican criminal justice system.

[60] *Informe Preliminar,* p. 23.

difficulty. The interrogations were conducted for the most part on unauthorized premises: military barracks; municipal agencies; churches; schools; etc.-- as well as in buildings belonging to local landowners and merchants-- rather than at police installations. During interrogations and subsequent transfer of prisoners to Tuxtla Gutiérrez, the army failed to inform relatives of the whereabouts of detainees.

In some municipalities, local authorities and ordinary civilians participated directly in illegal arrests. In these villages, animosities had been bubbling for years between the PRI municipal authorities and opposition citizens' groups, which accused officials of misusing public funds, corruption, and abuse. The case of Oxchuc is illustrative.

Oxchuc. Oxchuc is a small Tzeltal market town some twenty miles from San Cristóbal de las Casas on the road toward Altamirano. Its forty-eight Tzeltal-speaking communities are divided between supporters of the mayor, a member of the PRI, and an opposition citizens' association known as Los Tres Nudos ("The Three Knots," a Spanish translation of the Tzeltal word Oxchuc).[61]

Eleven suspected Zapatistas were caught and beaten by an angry mob of townspeople in Oxchuc on January 5, some three days after the EZLN had briefly occupied the town. The municipal authorities accused the EZLN of looting, vandalism, and kidnapping. The bloodied captives, who narrowly avoided lynching, were left trussed to a kiosk in the main square, where some of them were interviewed by reporters. They were later

---

[61] According to Tim Golden of the *New York Times*, who was present in Oxchuc, the PRI town council was voted in unanimously in the last election. Tres Nudos members allege that they were kept from the polls by threats and thrown rocks. Tim Golden, "Mexican Army is Said to Abuse Rebel Suspects," *New York Times*, January 24, 1994.

handed over to the police.[62] According to members of Tres Nudos, the mayor had previously broadcast a call through the kiosk's loudspeakers calling on the citizenry to arm themselves with guns, machetes, and staves and to assemble in the square. The crowd's hostility was directed mainly at Tres Nudos, whose supporters were publicly denounced by the mayor as EZLN supporters.

On January 15 and 16, municipal police, led by the mayor, detained sixteen members of Tres Nudos, blindfolded them, took them to a property belonging to the mayor, and later handed them over to the army. Feliciano Rodríguez Santiz, one of the detainees, told HRW/Americas in February that he saw the mayor passing money to an officer. The detainees were taken by army trucks and helicopters to Tuxtla Gutiérrez, where they were handed over to officials of the federal Attorney General's office, interrogated for two days, and then released without charge. They did not return to their communities for fear of further reprisals and went to a church refuge in San Cristóbal de las Casas.

On January 20, Feliciano López Santiz was detained in his home for the second time by army troops, this time with his son, Eliseo López Santiz. They were tied, blindfolded, and accused of giving shelter to Zapatistas and being leaders of Tres Nudos. They were released without charge after being held incommunicado for two days. On the following day, the army entered the community with sixteen vehicles and surrounded the houses where the Tres Nudos members were hiding. When the troops left that afternoon, the mayor threatened to expel all the Tres Nudos members and burn their houses by nightfall. Some 200 of the villagers abandoned the community fearing for their lives, and went to refuges in San Cristóbal.[63]

---

[62] Elio Henríquez, Ricardo Alemán and David Aponte, "Integran Tzeltales de Oxchuc un grupo de autodefensa contra más ataques rebeldes," *La Jornada,* January 6, 1994, p. 6.

[63] CONPAZ, *Primer Reporte de la Comisión de Derechos Humanos-CONPAZ,* March 21, 1994, pp. 11-12.

The Ministry of Defense confirmed the army's role in the illegal arrest of these villagers, stating that they handed over the sixteen "transgressors" to the federal Attorney General's office after other villagers had apprehended them for acts of vandalism.[64] However, this could not be considered a citizen's arrest since none of the detainees were captured while committing an offense. Tres Nudos denounced the abductions and alleged theft of property by the army to the Peace Commission. The mayor of Oxchuc was summoned for an interview in the state governor's office, and a state government official ordered a full investigation by the Public Ministry.

On April 15, CNDH staff members, as well as state government officials and members of the Mexican Red Cross, escorted one hundred and twenty-six families, who had been temporarily housed in the National Indigenous Institute (INI) refuge in San Cristóbal, back to their homes in Oxchuc.

To our knowledge, no charges have been made against either the civilians responsible for the abductions, or against the army for its complicity.

The army mounted similar raids in other communities suspected of harboring or supporting insurgents, in particular, Chanal, Huixtan, and Morelia.[65] Unlike Ocosingo, Altamirano, and Las Margaritas, these villages did not see serious fighting in the early days of the insurrection. Rather, like Oxchuc, the EZLN had briefly occupied them to muster support and then left. As in Oxchuc, the army collaborated closely with local PRI government officials or other civilians, who helped identify and round up suspects, and in some cases beat them and then ran them out of town.

---

[64] "SEDENA: Habitantes de Oxchuc entregaron a 16 transgresores, *La Jornada,* January 18, 1994.

[65] The events in Morelia are described in detail in Chapter VI.

45

Chanal. On January 6, army troops entered the village of Chanal, which had been held for five days by the EZLN after fighting in which at least two policemen and a civilian were killed. The army conducted house-to-house searches and detained fourteen men who had been pointed out by the mayor. Presumably the men were suspected as collaborators or supporters of the EZLN, whose combatants had left town by the time the army arrived. They were beaten, tied by the wrists and ankles and bundled into an army truck. The same day the army took them to the military base of Rancho Nuevo, where they were interrogated and then flown by helicopter to an army base in Tuxtla Gutiérrez. There the interrogations continued, allegedly accompanied by the application of electrical shocks, and the men were not presented to the PGR until January 12, six days after their arrest.

After questioning by the PGR, the men were released without charge and had to beg for money in the street to pay for their fare to San Cristóbal. On their return to Chanal, the mayor, Martín Pérez Díaz, assembled the villagers, denounced the men again and incited the villagers to beat them, allegedly beating two of them himself. The fourteen, together with their families, were expelled from the village that day and took refuge in a nearby community, where their testimonies were taken.[66]

Ejido Lázaro Cárdenas (Chilil), Huixtan. On the morning of January 8, an army convoy entered the ejido Lázaro Cárdenas, and spotted one of the *ejidatarios*, Manuel Alvarez Martínez, as he was leaving his home carrying a bag. The army opened fire on him, apparently believing that he was armed, and he ran back into his home. The troops fanned out and began searching homes for insurgents and weapons, making all the men lie on the floor at gunpoint. While two villagers, Manuel Moshan Culej and Miguel Martínez Huet were working on a latrine in their backyard, the soldiers found a single-shot .22-caliber rifle in Moshan's home. The three men were detained, blindfolded, and

---

[66] CONPAZ, "Torturados y Expulsados de Chanal," Communicado No. 23, February 5, 1994.

46

beaten. They were held overnight at Rancho Nuevo and, on the following day, taken by helicopter to a building in an army base in Tuxtla Gutiérrez, where they joined eighteen other detainees. During the night of January 9, they were blindfolded again and taken to the PGR headquarters in the city, where they were fed. The next day the judicial police interrogated the three men and asked them to sign declarations which they could not fully understand, since they were read in Spanish. On January 13, they were released without charge, together with eighteen other detainees (including the fourteen from Chanal). Manuel Martínez had to sell his watch to buy them a ticket home.[67]

Enrique Pérez López. Arbitrary arrests were also reported during the wave of land occupations which began immediately after the Zapatista uprising. Enrique Pérez López, President of the *Asociación de Derechos Humanos Sur-Sureste de Comitán* (South-South Eastern Human Rights Association of Comitán), was abducted at 12:45 pm on April 10 by a group of heavily armed ranchers at a property known as La Piedad, near Chicomuselo. Pérez, who had gone to witness a contract on behalf of fifty landless peasants who were trying to buy some disputed land, was cornered, together with the peasants, by some forty-five men brandishing automatic weapons, and whose faces were covered by bandannas. The men insulted and threatened the peasants, fired warning shots into the air, and then bundled Pérez and the peasants into trucks and drove away.

The convoy of some twenty vehicles stopped along the road and the ranchers released the peasants, all of whom had been unarmed except for their machetes. Pérez's captors confiscated his credentials, beat him, and drove him to a ranch known as Las Florecitas, where they repeatedly threatened to kill him. Pérez told HRW/Americas that one of the leaders of the group, who scarcely spoke and kept apart from the rest, had a military appearance and bearing and did not look like a rancher.

---

[67] The three men gave detailed testimonies to the editor of the San Cristóbal de las Casas daily, *El Tiempo*.

After warning Peréz not to denounce what had occurred, the ranchers handed him over to the municipal police in Chicomuselo, who held him on suspicions of criminal association and destruction of property (*despojo*). On April 11, after spending the night in jail in Chicomuselo, he was taken to Comitán and on the following day questioned by the Public Ministry. During the afternoon, some two hundred ranchers surrounded the Public Ministry building, shouting for Pérez to be charged, and threatened to burn the car of officials of the CNDH who were also present. On April 14, Pérez was summoned before the judge. The ranchers surrounded the courtroom. Evidently acting under pressure, the judge charged Pérez with destruction of property and set bail at 16,000 nuevos pesos (approximately $5,000), an amount which neither he nor the peasants were able to pay. Pérez was taken to No. 10 prison in Comitán. While he was in prison, the ranchers told his wife and 86-year-old mother, who lived with him, that the army would come in the night and evict them.

Pérez said that the declaration he made and signed before the secretary of the Public Ministry was subsequently tampered with. A sentence was inserted in his statement to the effect that the peasants involved in the incident with the ranchers had been armed.[68]

The Comitán Hunger Strike. Enrique Pérez's case is illustrative of the abuses which continue to affect the penal system in Mexico's rural areas, and of which the victims, in many cases, are poor Indian farmers. Although the present chapter is dedicated to abuses committed during the war against those suspected of connection with the Zapatistas, it should not be forgotten that the due process rights of Indian suspects, whatever

---

[68] "*Enrique Pérez López declara y acepta que los campesinos con que se encontraba portaban armas preveniendo de cualquier agresión que sufrieran.*" Enrique Pérez López declares and accepts that the peasants he was with were carrying weapons as a precaution against any attack to which they might be subject.

the crime, have been ignored and circumvented for years, even under "normal" peacetime conditions.

On May 16, with Enrique Pérez's encouragement, thirty-eight prisoners held in the Comitán prison went on an indefinite hunger strike to protest abuses by the justice and prison authorities which had led to their indefinite imprisonment on what they insisted were false charges. Pérez told HRW/Americas that most of the 110 prisoners he met in Comitán prison had stories of corruption and injustice similar to his own, including the fabrication and falsification of affidavits.

On the third day of the strike, in what appears to have been an attempt to defuse the protest, an appeals court judge reduced Pérez's bail to 3,000 pesos and paid it himself. Pérez was then released. In the following weeks, fourteen of the other hunger strikers were released. The federal Attorney General's office either dropped their prosecutions, or they were granted pardons or parole. On June 6, the remaining twenty-four strikers were visited by the state governor, Javier López Moreno, accompanied by the president of the state Appeals Court.[69] By June 22, all but eight had been released, after their cases had been reviewed by a group which included Pérez himself, and representatives of the CEOIC, the CNDH, and the Chiapas state human rights commission. The review group found that the rights of all but six prisoners had been violated.

---

[69] All but five of the prisoners rejected the governor's appeal to suspend their strike in return for a reply to their demands within five days. According to Enrique Pérez, who visited the president of the Appeals Court, Arturo Nazar Sevilla, the following day, the judge said that because of the prisoners' defiance, the governor's offer had been withdrawn. He said, "What we need is for two of the prisoners to die of hunger so that there are no hunger strikes in other Chiapas prisons." The five men who accepted the governor's offer were not released within five days either. José Gil Olmos, "Que mueran dos para que escarmienten: Nazar Sevilla," *El Tiempo*, June 9, 1994.

Following investigations conducted by the state human rights commission, three state justice officials were reportedly dismissed. They included an official of the Public Ministry who was alleged to have forged Pérez's declaration, a court-appointed defense attorney, who was alleged to have "arranged" prisoners' defenses in the interest of third parties, and the director of Comitán prison No. 10.[70]

Torture and Ill-Treatment

Virtually all of the Indians detained as suspects by the Mexican army were ill-treated.[71] In many cases, detainees were brutally beaten at the moment of arrest and during subsequent interrogation. Prisoners were bound tightly by hand and foot, blindfolded, and restrained for long periods while being transported from one place to another. Many detainees reported being given no food or water for several days. By most accounts, treatment improved only when they were handed over to justice officials of the PGR; at which time, the detainees were untied, given food and water often for the first time, received a medical examination, and were appointed a defense lawyer.

Other detainees were subjected to gross physical torture, including being submerged in barrels of water and having carbonated water forced up their nasal passages, both of which produce near-asphyxiation. A number of people credibly alleged that they had been tortured with electric shock. Some testified that soldiers had threatened to kill them or throw them out of helicopters transporting them for interrogation.

---

[70] "Cesan al Director del Penal de Comitán," *El Tiempo*, June 22, 1994.

[71] Dozens of testimonies of torture and other forms of abuse were published in the press and collected by Mexican nongovernmental human rights groups, as well as other international delegations which visited Chiapas.

In February, the CNDH released its first findings on the treatment of detainees. It stated that of 131 detainees visited by commissioners in Cerro Hueco prison, and whose testimonies were recorded on videotape, seventy-two had light injuries and six had serious injuries.[72] The CNDH concluded:

> It is indisputable that these people were ill-treated, which makes it imperative to find those members of the army, the public security, and judicial police forces responsible. The complaints lodged with CNDH are associated with other violations, such as illegal arrest, incommunication, false accusations, and also in some cases, torture, although the latter has not been proven.[73]

The following is a small sample of the prisoners whose injuries were recorded by CNDH's medical team. The brief case descriptions include extracts of testimonies collected, not by the CNDH, but by nongovernmental organizations belonging to the National Network of Nongovernmental Human Rights Organizations, which visited the PGR headquarters in Tuxtla Gutiérrez in February, and by HRW/Americas during a visit to Cerro Hueco prison during the same month.

● *Celestino López Pérez*: "I was arrested in Barrio Nuevo, Chalán, while we were meeting with the bosses and they took us to the barracks at Rancho Nuevo, and we were three days and

---

[72] The CNDH uses the Mexican forensic distinction between wounds "which are nonlife-threatening and heal within fifteen days," and wounds "which are life-threatening, and take more than fifteen days to heal."

[73] Comisión Nacional de Derechos Humanos, "Informe Especial a la Opinión Pública sobre las Actividades y Consideraciones de la Comisión Nacional de Derechos Humanos en el Caso de los Altos y la Selva de Chiapas," Mexico, February 22, 1994. In its Annual Report (1994), the CNDH said it had received seventy-six complaints of torture in cases related to the conflict, *Programa Permanente de la CNDH en los Altos y Selva de Chiapas*, June 13, 1994, p. 622.

nights without a drop of water or any food, and they were torturing us. They put water in our mouths and noses until we almost drowned and others beat us on the heart or kicked us, pretty bad, and we had had nothing to eat." Ramón Morales Enzin, detained with Celestino López, alleges that he received the same treatment.

● *Manuel Moshán Culej, Miguel Martínez Uet,* and *Manuel Martínez Uet,* detained in Huixtan were stripped, bound hand and foot, and dunked repeatedly in a tank of water at the Rancho Nuevo military base. Manuel Moshán said he lost consciousness, and when he recovered he was beaten and his head repeatedly smashed against the wall. "I had trouble bearing the cold, because they left me to sleep on the floor with my hands tied."

● *Celestino Rodríguez Gómez:* "I was in my house when the soldier came. 'Let's go,' he said. I said, 'I haven't done anything wrong.' 'And those trousers? (they were green),' the soldier asked. I told him they are from Chanal and that I had bought them almost a year ago. 'You're a Zapatista,' said the soldier, and he started to hit me. Later, I was taken to Rancho Nuevo."[74]

● *Alberto Alvarez, Nicolás Martínez, Julián Gómez, Nicolás Albores* and *Elías Gómez* were among a group of eighteen peasants detained during the first week of January in Ocosingo. The HRW/Americas investigator, who interviewed the group in Cerro Hueco in February, noted purple weals on their wrists consistent with the use of tight ligatures. Elías Gómez also had facial bruises and a scar on his head, which he said was due to a blow from a rifle butt.

● *Pedro Hernández Jiménez* and *Benancio Hernández Jiménez,* brothers from Altamirano, were detained in their home

---

[74] The above testimonies are from an unpublished document by the National Network of Non-Governmental Human Rights Organizations. The testimonies were taken on January 10, 1994.

on January 9. They told HRW/Americas that while held in an army base in Tuxtla Gutiérrez, they were given electric shocks on the chest and legs from an instrument they described as a "small black box" to which cables were attached (presumably a battery). Benancio Hernández was ordered to put on an EZLN uniform and then photographed. He showed the HRW/Americas investigator dark violet marks on his legs which appeared consistent with electric shock torture.[75]

- *Francisco Gómez Santiz* was detained in Altamirano on January 11 while his wife was claiming emergency assistance from the army. He was bound hand and foot, blindfolded, and thrown into a vehicle. He said:

> They took me in a helicopter with several people.
> We were not allowed to talk. They told us several
> times that they were taking us to the Sumidero
> Canyon and that they were going to throw us out
> in the air. The soldiers beat us with the tips of
> their rifles, and when we reached Tuxtla they gave
> us electric shocks on the neck and shoulder.[76]

- *María Teresa Méndez Sánchez, Cristina Méndez Sánchez and María Méndez Sánchez.* The Méndez Sánchez sisters, aged 20, 18, and 16 respectively, are Tzeltal residents of Morelia, who were detained by the army on June 4. The sisters were returning with their mother to the community of Santa Rosita Sibaquil after selling produce in Altamirano. After being refused passage at an army roadblock, they took an alternative route home, but were again stopped at a another roadblock at about 2:00 pm. The three sisters were separated from their mother and taken to a wooden hut, where they were held for some two and a half hours.

---

[75] An Amnesty International physician who examined him on January 21 told HRW/Americas that he saw clear physical evidence to confirm Pedro Hernández's account of torture.

[76] CONPAZ, Comunicado No. 12, January 19, 1994.

During this time, they were questioned, accused of being Zapatistas, and allegedly kicked and beaten with rifle butts. The women later testified that they were then raped by some thirty soldiers who entered and left the hut, until an officer intervened and stopped them. The women were threatened with death or imprisonment if they denounced what had happened. After the case received publicity in the national press, the officer responsible for Altamirano promised to investigate, and the CNDH also began an investigation of its own.[77]

Disturbing allegations were made subsequently about the manner in which the CNDH conducted its investigation of the incident. Two CNDH investigators reportedly visited the community on June 21. Unable to obtain information from adults whom they questioned as to the whereabouts of the women, the officials paid two children money to point out the house where the women were staying. To gain the confidence of the women, who were alone in the house, the CNDH officials reportedly posed as members of CHILTAK, a local nongovernmental agency which works in Indian communities and is known and trusted by locals. After questioning the women, they drafted a document whose contents the women were unable to understand since they could not read or write. "At the end of the document they put our names, and one of them held our hands and pressed our thumbs onto a pad, and the other pressed our thumbs onto the piece of paper he was holding. They told us it was so that what we had said should have more legal weight."[78]

CONPAZ and the San Cristóbal de las Casas Womens Group lodged a criminal complaint against the soldiers allegedly

---

[77] Jose Gil Olmos, "Denuncian violación por 30 soldados, 3 mujeres tzeltales," *La Jornada*, June 17, 1994; José Gil Olmos, "El ejército investigará la violación a las mujeres de Morelia," *El Tiempo*, June 19, 1994.

[78] Elio Henríquez and José Gil Olmos, "Pide la CNDH constatar la objetividad de sus evidencias," *La Jornada,* July 2, 1994.

involved in the rape, as well as against the CNDH officials. The case is still under investigation.

Due Process: Peasants Imprisoned as Presumed Zapatistas

"Our misfortune and our crime is to have been neighbors or natives of the place where the events occurred. We have to live somewhere on this earth. Who saw any one of us fire a weapon against another human being?"
> -- Twenty-one prisoners held as Zapatistas, Cerro Hueco prison, in a letter to President Salinas, March 29, 1994, as they started a hunger strike for their release.

"When we were before the district judge, still afraid but speaking a bit more freely, we told what had really happened. Some explained that they participated in the rebellion because they were tricked. Others said that they were detained because they were unlucky enough to live in the conflict zone, and others because they were foolhardy and went to see what was happening in our towns, or left their homes to buy necessities. We had the misfortune to run into the Mexican Army, which proceeded to arrest us without any investigation."
> -- Zapatista prisoner interviewed by reporters, April 5, 1994.[79]

---

[79] David Aponte, José Antonio Román and Elio Henríquez, "Evalua la CNDH la acción judicial contra 21 presuntos Zapatistas," *La Jornada*, April 5, 1994.

*"I wrote immediately to Mr. Hans López Muñoz,
the first district judge, to repeat that you do not
belong, nor have ever belonged to our EZLN."*
-- Subcomandante Marcos in a letter to the
remaining five prisoners detained during the
conflict, May 8, 1994.

Approximately seventy people, detained during the first
two weeks of January, were charged under state and federal
jurisdiction with criminal offenses arising out of the Zapatista
rebellion. The thirty-eight state law prisoners were released
during the second week of February, on bond or conditional
liberty, leaving thirty-two federal law prisoners still in detention.

On February 13, the HRW/Americas representative visited
Cerro Hueco prison in Tuxtla Gutiérrez and spoke to twenty-eight
of these prisoners, who were from Ocosingo, Altamirano,
Morelia, and San Miguel Chiptik. All were being held for
"murder," "causing injuries," "criminal association," and
"carrying arms exclusively reserved for the armed forces." They
denied the charges categorically, and said they were not members
of the Zapatista army. Most of the prisoners said they were
arrested in their homes, or after venturing out into the street.
They complained of beatings and threats during interrogation and
said that the federal prosecutor forced them to sign a statement
that they were not allowed to see. No lawyer was provided.

All the prisoners were being held on the same four
charges listed above. This suggested that the prosecutor had
insufficient evidence on which to base individual prosecutions and
was pressing the charges indiscriminately. None of the prisoners
knew the name of the person he allegedly killed or wounded, and
they said the name did not feature in the prosecution evidence
either. All of them denied they were carrying weapons when
arrested, or that prohibited weapons were discovered in their
homes. According to a reporter who reviewed the case dossiers,
the charges did not name any victims, and the prosecution file
lacked death certificates or hospital reports of injuries,
photographs of bodies or other forensic evidence, autopsy reports

or ballistics tests. The case against the men seems to have rested mainly on evidence given by soldiers. The circumstances in which the prisoners' extrajudicial statements were taken by army interrogators would make that evidence inadmissable under Mexican law, unless confirmed before a judge.[80]

On March 29, the twenty-one prisoners still in detention began a hunger strike for their release. As the protest gathered force in April, a CNDH official told reporters that the Commission was investigating the prisoners' allegations of ill-treatment and the action of the Public Ministry, and would subsequently give its findings. On April 14, the CNDH sent recommendations to the PGR, requesting that the charges against sixteen of the hunger-strikers be withdrawn. These prisoners were released on April 18 and transported by the CNDH back to their communities.[81]

Marcos Morales Cruz, a photographer from Ocosingo who had been detained on January 3, told his story in an interview with reporters from the San Cristóbal daily, *El Tiempo*:

> The soldiers came to protect the people, not to harm them. That's why I went into the street at dawn on Monday. I had stayed in my house and when I went out to buy tortillas I saw lots of people. On my way back, over by the Cruz Blanca pharmacy I was arrested. There were soldiers in the building and they called me over. "Come over here," they shouted. I thought they wanted me to do something for them, but when I went in they grabbed my arms and clubbed me with their rifle butts. "Where did you go?" they asked me. I said I had been to Coplamar (a

---

[80] Jaime Avilés, "Zapatistas de Cerro Hueco, torturados con la incomunicación," *El Tiempo,* March 12, 1994.

[81] CNDH, "Programa Permanante de la CNDH en los Altos y Selva de Chiapas," *Informe Anual*, 1994, June 13, 1994, p. 625-626.

cooperative store), where my family were. "What Coplamar? We're going to screw you (*te vamos a chingar*), you went into a house and changed your clothes, you are a Zapatista." They punched me, blindfolded me, hit me in the eye with a rifle butt, but what hurt most was a blow from a rifle butt in my back when one of them got on top of me...

Morales was one of thirty-five detainees who were first held in the partially destroyed town hall, and then transferred to a warehouse owned by a civilian, Tito Méndez. Two days after his arrest, Morales was taken back to his home where the soldiers confiscated his camera, enlarger, laboratory equipment, and film stock. By mid-May Mendez still had not received his equipment back and was unable to practice his trade. He decided to write to President Carlos Salinas about his case.[82]

The day before Morales' arrest, his father, Miguel Morales Méndez, was killed in crossfire near the Mexican Institute of Social Security hospital. His body was exhumed by the CNDH from a common grave in the town cemetery and identified by his other son (see Chapter VI).

Deaths Resulting from Excessive Use of Force

PHR and HRW/Americas are concerned about two cases in which army troops appear to have used excessive force. The first involves a fatal incident in which soldiers opened fire on a "Combi," or van, which had failed to stop at a checkpoint near the army base in Rancho Nuevo, killing four passengers, including a child, and injuring five others. All of the victims were civilians. The other case, which also took place near the army base, involves at least ten Zapatistas and four civilians who were ambushed in a minibus by soldiers.

---

[82] José Gil Olmos and Elio Henríquez, "Los Zapatistas no los hicieron daño, pero el ejército sí," *El Tiempo*, May 26, 1994.

The Minibus Incident. After arriving in Oxchuc on January 2, EZLN members used the town's speaker system to summon the residents to a meeting in the town square. Among those who went to the square that morning was a 14-year-old boy named Enrique Santiz Gómez:

> I went down there with my father [Pablo Santiz Gómez] and my brother [Uber] to listen to what the Zapatistas had to say. As we were leaving the square, a local guy who was standing with a group of about thirty Zapatistas pointed to my father and said that he owned a minibus and knew how to drive. The Zapatistas accompanied us to our house, where my mother was waiting for us. My father told my older brother, Uber, to get the minibus, and we all climbed on board. The Zapatistas said that we were going to Huixtan. But when we arrived at a nearby shop, the rebels made me get off the bus as more Zapatistas climbed on. With them were two other men who weren't Zapatistas. I then walked home.

Other witnesses who saw Pablo Santiz Gómez, aged 35, and his son, Uber, aged 18, leave with the rebels were his young wife, Josefa, and another son, Mario. It was the last time the father and son were seen alive.

On January 3, journalists discovered the minibus riddled with bullets on the side of the road near the army base at Rancho Nuevo. About seven meters from the vehicle lay the bodies of fourteen men, most of them dressed in Zapatista uniforms. Later, Josefa, in the presence of PGR investigators, identified the bodies of her husband and stepson and the minibus, with its license plate number 386 HC2, from photographs taken by reporters (see photographs) at the scene. She also identified the two men among the bodies taken to the morgue in Tuxtla Gutiérrez. Relatives of the other two civilians--Cesar Méndez Gómez and Fernando Santiz Gómez--also identified them from scene photographs.

Although the minibus incident appears, at first, to have been an army ambush, there are several troubling aspects about the case that need to be clarified. If it was an ambush, why, as journalists have reported, were no spent cartridge shells found inside the minibus? And why were the bodies found lying outside the vehicle? Were the men attempting to flee? Were they forced out at gunpoint? Or, after the ambush, did army troops drag the corpses out of the vehicle? If, as several witnesses claim, there were approximately thirty Zapatistas and civilians on the minibus when it left Oxchuc, why were only fourteen corpses found next to the vehicle? And, finally, was the fusillade so intense that no one on the minibus survived the attack?

There is another aspect of the case which needs to be clarified: In a press bulletin of April 7, the PGR claimed that Pablo Santiz Gómez was one of five men summarily executed in the marketplace of Ocosingo on January 2 (see Chapter VI). Such a claim contradicts all the known facts (see photographs). To begin with, Pablo Santiz Gómez was last seen on the minibus leaving Oxchuc. According to several witnesses, he appeared to go willingly with the Zapatistas or, at least, no one recalls hearing the Zapatistas threaten him. Santiz's wife and other relatives identified his body among the corpses found lying next to the bus. Photographs taken of the corpses by the vehicle show Santiz's body with boots on, as does the morgue photograph of his body taken in Tuxtla Gutiérrez. However, in the photographs taken of the five bodies in the Ocosingo marketplace, only one body is shown wearing one boot (see photos). And it is unlikely that those recovering the five bodies put footwear back onto the bodies. Finally, on the death certificate for Pablo Santiz Gómez, the PGR gives the place of death as along the "stretch of road between San Cristóbal and Oxchuc," not in Ocosingo.

HRW/Americas and PHR have written to the federal Attorney General regarding the contradictory findings in the minibus incident, but have received no reply. In June 1994, then-Attorney General Diego Valadéz refused to meet with a representative of HRW/Americas in Mexico City to discuss the case.

The CNDH states it has identified all fourteen victims found by the minibus, but it has not been able to clarify the circumstances in which they died. The CNDH's account does not refer to the questioning of civilian witnesses, if there were any, nor does it mention what response, if any, the Ministry of National Defense gave to the CNDH's requests for information.[83]

The Combi Incident. On January 4, at about 6:00 pm, army troops opened fire on a Volkswagen bus, or "Combi," moments after it ran through a military checkpoint fifty meters from the army base in Rancho Nuevo. Four of the nine persons in the vehicle were killed, including a young girl, and five others were badly injured.

The following morning, journalists photographed the bullet-ridden vehicle in the company of several soldiers. By then, only two bodies remained inside the van: one body was sprawled across the floor near the middle seat, and another, reportedly a male passenger who had been seated next to the driver, was stretched, face down, across the front seat with his legs hanging out of the open door on the driver's side. On the front seat, next to the man's outstretched hand, was a pistol (see photograph).

In June 1994, the CNDH released a summary of its preliminary findings in the case:

> In its investigation of the [Combi incident], the CNDH has taken testimonies from most of the injured, from which it can be concluded that the owner and driver of the vehicle was forced by the passenger beside him not to stop at the checkpoint. The passenger stepped on the vehicle's accelerator causing it to swerve toward the soldiers who were waiting to inspect the vehicle. Although these circumstances seem clear, it is likely that the

---

[83] Comisión Nacional de Derechos Humanos, "Programa Permanente de la CNDH en Los Altos y Selva de Chiapas," *Informe mayo de 1993 - mayo de 1994,* pp. 643-644.

position in which this particular passenger was killed was different from the body's position in the photograph that has been widely circulated. The CNDH has reached this conclusion partly because of the inconsistencies between the location of the wounds on the body and the absence of blood stains on the back of the seat in which the body was supposedly found and photographed and partly because of the presence of grass in the clothes and hair of the deceased. It would seem that the body was deliberately placed in this position, which was the one analyzed by the CNDH's investigators.[84]

The CNDH's conclusion that one of the passengers forced the vehicle to run the checkpoint may be correct. However, one of the survivors, Agustín Ruiz Guzmán, views the series of events differently:

> I got on the Combi in Comitán at about 5:30 in the evening. I took a seat in the back. At that point, there were four of us, including the driver, on board. A little further down the road, the driver stopped to pick up more passengers. I remember he told them to hurry up because it was getting dark and there were Zapatistas in the area. The driver then took off, driving as fast as he could. I was dozing when I suddenly heard the other passengers screaming at the driver to stop. When I looked up, I saw one of the passengers grabbing at the steering wheel, as if he was trying to get the driver to pull over and stop.[85]

---

[84] *Ibid.*, pp. 636-637.

[85] PHR representatives interviewed Agustín Ruiz Guzmán in San Cristóbal on March 29, 1994.

Ruiz believes that no one in the Combi had any intention of running through the checkpoint. He says it was an accident: it was getting dark, and the driver, who was nervous and speeding on a bad stretch of road, didn't see the checkpoint in time. The Combi was then hit with a hail of bullets.

> I can't remember exactly, but it seemed like the shooting lasted maybe five or ten minutes. The Combi came to a stop on the side of the road, with its front wheels in a drainage ditch. I felt a pain in my side. A baby, maybe seven months old or so, had fallen between my legs and was crying. Her mother was sitting next to me and was also wounded...When the shooting stopped, the driver stuck his hands out the window and started shouting, 'Don't shoot! We're all civilians! We're just passengers! Don't shoot!' But they started firing again. Only this time, it was sporadic. A burst of fire. Silence. And then another burst. I was hit again, and the pain was incredible.

Ruiz believes that a grenade was also thrown at the back of the vehicle, just under the rear bumper, but that it didn't explode properly. He recalls hearing an explosion and then feeling glass crashing down on his head and shoulders.

Soldiers eventually approached the vehicle and opened the side door, shouting for everyone not to move, and if they had weapons, to throw them out. "They took the women beside me out, and then the baby," Ruiz recalls. "I got out next, and could see that they had taken all the passengers out and laid them on the ground next to the vehicle." Ruiz showed an officer his laboratory identification card. He explained that, through his job, he had come to know some of the medics at the base, and asked if he could see them.

The military transferred the wounded to Tuxtla Gutiérrez. Ruiz, the passenger next to him Petrona López Gómez, and her baby were taken to the military hospital. Four days later, Ruiz was transferred to a civilian clinic and then released.

López, who lost her husband, father, and eight-year-old sister during the assault on the Combi, says that military personnel at the hospital asked her to keep quiet about the incident.[86] Ruiz, too, was warned. He says that shortly after his discharge from the hospital, an army officer approached him at his father's house in San Cristóbal de las Casas. The officer, who was a friend of his father, advised him to forget about the incident and not to talk to about it to anyone, especially the CNDH as they were out to slander the Mexican armed forces. At the time of writing, October 1994, no disciplinary measures have been taken against army personnel in connection with the Combi incident.

---

[86] Hugo Robles Guillén, "Los soldados simplemente nos dispararon," *El Tiempo*, San Cristóbal de las Casas, June 10, 1994, p. 1.

VI. INVESTIGATIONS OF EXTRAJUDICIAL EXECUTIONS

In the days following the military offensive against EZLN forces, accounts of alleged extrajudicial, arbitrary, and summary executions [86] of Zapatistas and civilians by the Mexican army were reported widely in the national and international media. The first case to receive notoriety was the apparent execution-style killing of five men in the marketplace of Ocosingo during the military's siege of that town on January 2.

Weeks later, journalists reported the discovery of a mass grave in the Ocosingo cemetery.

On January 7, in the isolated ejido of Morelia, army troops reportedly from the Cabalería Motorizada de Comitán detained and tortured three men whose bodies later appeared in a ravine six kilometers from the village. According to villagers, the army officers who detained the men made a public spectacle of the victims' bodies after torture.

Another case, which drew less public attention, was the murder of two young men in Las Margaritas soon after their arrest by police on January 16. Eight days later, a man hunting on the outskirts of town found the bodies of the two men, bearing multiple stab wounds.

Despite the Mexican government's repeated pledges to bring perpetrators of human rights abuses to justice promptly, no

---

[86] Extrajudicial (or extralegal), arbitrary, and summary executions include: (a) political assassinations; (b) deaths resulting from torture or ill-treatment in prison or detention; (c) death resulting from enforced "disappearances"; (d) deaths resulting from the excessive use of force by law-enforcement personnel; (e) executions without due process; and (f) acts of genocide. See "Principles on the Effective Prevention and Investigation of Extralegal, Arbitrary, and Summary Executions," adopted by the United Nations Economic and Social Council, Resolution 1989/65, May 24, 1989, p. 3.

one has been charged in connection with any of these cases. Furthermore, there are signs that criminal investigations have either been deliberately bungled to protect the Mexican army from being held culpable, or conducted with an astonishing lack of professional rigor.

Under the Mexican Constitution, the *Ministerio Público* (district attorney or public ministry), is responsible for investigating and prosecuting homicides. Within the public ministry, the agent or prosecutor assigned to a case is responsible to the state Attorney General's office for investigation and prosecution of offenses under the state penal code, and to the federal Attorney General (PGR) for the prosecution of federal offenses. The federal Attorney General's Office, which is responsible to the executive power, is the ultimate supervisory body for all federal Public Ministry Agents in the country. The Federal District Attorney General who covers Mexico City and each of the state Attorneys General are responsible for the Public Ministries under their jurisdiction.

In most of the cases discussed here, state and federal agencies have sent criminal investigators and forensic scientists to interview witnesses and gather and examine evidence. The CNDH, in its role as government ombudsman, has also fielded teams of criminologists, forensic scientists, and investigators. In at least three of the cases--the summary executions in the Ocosingo marketplace, the mass grave in Ocosingo, and the torture and murder of three men from Morelia--the *Procurador General de Justicia Militar*, or military prosecutor, General Mario Guillermo Fromow García, has assigned special investigators to determine whether military personnel were implicated in these killings.

Since January 1994, HRW/Americas and PHR have conducted their own investigations of these cases, including interviews with witnesses, government officials and forensic scientists, human rights advocates, and relatives of the deceased. For the first four months of 1994, PHR maintained a representative, Dr. Thomas Crane, in San Cristóbal de las Casas.

During that time, Dr. Crane and several PHR forensic scientists observed autopsies, examined postmortem reports and photographs, and visited crime scenes.

PHR and HRW/Americas are concerned that the PGR, which is the government agency primarily responsible for investigating the cases described below, has often shown greater interest in protecting the Mexican army's reputation than in conducting independent and thorough investigations. We believe the evidence indicates that the PGR has tried to cover up possible military involvement in the summary execution of five men in the Ocosingo marketplace on January 2, 1994. Moreover, the CNDH's integrity has been badly tarnished by its reluctance to speak out in a forceful and timely manner when it has been aware of incompetence, discrepancies, or outright contradictions in the findings and conclusions drawn by the PGR.

At the time of writing, October 1994, no one has been charged in connection with the four cases described below. Nor, to our knowledge, has the CNDH issued any public recommendations on these cases to the PGR or any other government authority.

1. Five Summary Executions in the Ocosingo Marketplace

Zapatista forces entered the town of Ocosingo late in the evening on December 31, 1993. By early morning, nearly 400 rebels had gathered in the central plaza and were preparing to launch an assault on the Presidencia Municipal, or townhall. At 8:00 am, the rebels opened fire on twenty to thirty state judicial police who were inside the building. The battle lasted eight hours and left four police officers dead.

Once the rebels took control of the building, they set out to destroy it with mortars and sledgehammers. They ransacked municipal records and hurled them from the charred windows to the plaza below. They also broke into and looted the ISSTE (the Social Security Institution for State Employees) store.

At dawn on January 2, army units from the 17th, 53rd, and 73rd battalions based in Villahermosa, Tabasco, arrived in Ocosingo. Outnumbered and outgunned, the Zapatistas retreated. As they withdrew, they set fire to the municipal building and the office of the state Attorney General. They also destroyed installations of the judicial police and the state security police.[87]

As the army advanced, about 150 rebels took up positions in the marketplace several blocks south of the central plaza. By mid-afternoon, a major firefight raged through the market.[88] The surviving rebels eventually fled through the San Rafael neighborhood, only to be cut off by soldiers. At least twenty civilians were caught in the cross-fire, and dozens of Zapatistas were killed.

On the morning of January 3, military airplanes and helicopters appeared in the sky over Ocosingo, and soldiers began to set up checkpoints along the major roads into town. In the neighborhoods of San José, Linda Vista, and San Rafael, soldiers went from house to house searching for Zapatistas and their sympathizers. That night, the Secretary of National Defense announced on national television that the army had taken control of the towns of Ocosingo, San Cristóbal de las Casas, Altamirano, and Las Margaritas.

Reporters first toured Ocosingo on the morning of January 4. One reporter wrote that he had seen twenty-four corpses in the streets and markets, including the body of a child, and that the bodies of at least eight police and soldiers had been removed.[89]

---

[87] Matilde Pérez U. and Rosa Rojas, "Fuerte combate en Ocosingo entre soldados y el EZLN: version de 50 alzados muertos," *La Jornada*, January 3, 1994, p. 4.

[88] Ricardo Alemán, "Abandona Ocosingo y Altamirano el Ejército Zapatista de Liberación Nacional," *La Jornada*, January 5, 1994, p. 11.

[89] John Rice, "Locals emerge to bloodied town," *Miami Herald*, January 5, 1994.

Tim Golden of the *New York Times* described a grisly scene he and other journalists had discovered in the labyrinth of wooden and concrete stalls at the marketplace:

> At least a dozen rebels had been killed in and around the Ocosingo market. Six were found lying face down, shot at close range in the back of the head, their hands behind them and short lengths of nylon rope beside them. One still had his hands tied...[90]

Within hours, images of five of the bodies, lying one next to the other, appeared in newspapers and on television screens around the world.[91]

In the weeks following the discovery of the bodies, at least three agencies of the Mexican government and armed forces--the office of the PGR, CNDH, and the office of the military Judicial Prosecutor's office (PGJM)--announced that they had opened investigations into the deaths in the Ocosingo marketplace.

On January 7, the PGR, then under the leadership of Dr. Jorge Carpizo, released a press bulletin, stating that it had sent thirty forensic experts to Chiapas to investigate deaths resulting

---

[90] Tim Golden, "As Mexican Army Pursues Rebels, Fears Arise Over Rights Abuses," *New York Times*, January 6, 1994.

[91] The sixth body Golden refers to was some twenty meters away from the group of five bodies. Tod Robberson of the *Washington Post* described another disturbing scene in which a severely wounded rebel lay in a ditch with a pistol still at his side. He was breathing heavily but appeared to be unconscious and bleeding from the head. Soldiers nearby made no attempt to render first aid (see Chapter VII). *Televisa*, the national television network, aired a video of a brief interview with him. The man was later found dead. See Tod Robberson, "Rebels Pull Out of Towns as Mexican Army Mops Up," *The Washington Post*, January 5, 1994 and Jaime Avilés, "Después de la Fama, un Tiro en la Frente," *El Financiero*, January 6, 1994.

from the uprising. Two days earlier, according to the press advisory, federal agents had transported thirty bodies from Ocosingo to the state capital of Tuxtla Gutiérrez. On January 6, the agency's experts autopsied the Ocosingo bodies and concluded:

> Twenty-six of these bodies showed no indication of having received a gunshot wound with the characteristics attributed to what is called a "coup de grace"...In the four remaining bodies, which have gunshot wounds to the head, the studies and expert findings indicate the following: (a) The approximate time of death of one of the bodies was between forty-eight and seventy-two hours; another between twenty-four and thirty-six hours; another at more than seventy-two hours; and, finally, one at thirty-six hours. These findings clearly indicate that the moment of death [of these individuals] occurred on different days and at different times. (b) Based on the characteristics of the entrance wounds, they were short range gunshot wounds to the head. (c) Based on the size of the entrance wounds in two of the bodies, the wounds were not caused by high-powered weapons (the bullets had to have been .38-caliber or less), which is to say, the caliber was smaller than that of the restricted weapons used by the Armed Forces. (d) The characteristics of the wounds in a third body suggest that they were produced by a high-powered weapon, such as a .762 caliber or higher. (e) In a fourth body, the presence of metal fragments suggests that the gunshot wound to the head was produced by a scatter-shot weapon such as a shotgun--a weapon and ammunition not used by the Mexican army. These findings indicate that in three of the cases the possibility that the gunshot wounds originated from a member of the Mexican army can be dismissed, especially because they do not carry these types of weapons. In the case of the gunshot

70

wound produced by a high-powered weapon, it is not possible to specify, at this time, from whom it originated, especially as the armed and violent group also used this type of weapon. The investigation will continue to determine those presumed to be responsible.[92]

As the first official pronouncement on the apparent executions in Ocosingo, the PGR press statement raised more questions than answers. To begin with, the statement failed to mention whether clothing, spent cartridge shells or ligatures had been recovered at the crime scene--all of which were present in press photographs taken of the bodies (see photographs). There was also no mention of ligature marks on the bodies, nor whether they were dressed as civilians or wearing Zapatista uniforms. Moreover, journalists recalled seeing five to six bodies--not four-- laying face down in the stalls of the marketplace.

On January 21, two PHR forensic scientists--forensic anthropologist Clyde Collins Snow and forensic pathologist Margarita Arruza--arrived in Chiapas to assist Dr. Thomas Crane in an independent investigation of the Ocosingo case and other cases of apparent summary executions that had taken place during the uprising. The next evening, the PHR representatives met with CNDH president Jorge Madrazo in San Cristóbal de las Casas. In the meeting, Madrazo expressed doubts about the PGR's findings in the Ocosingo case and asked the two U.S. forensic scientists to examine some of the evidence and advise the CNDH.

Madrazo and the U.S. scientists met again the following evening. This time, they were accompanied by four CNDH forensic scientists. The CNDH scientists were eager to show Snow and Arruza press photographs of the crime scene and their own autopsy photographs of the five bodies found face down in the Ocosingo marketplace. It soon became clear that the PGR's

---

[92] Boletín de prensa, Procuraduría General de la República, January 7, 1994 (009/94).

71

experts had either autopsied the wrong bodies or had never seen the bodies from the Ocosingo market.

The CNDH scientists explained that at some point in the investigation the state (as opposed to the federal) Attorney General's office had removed and stored the clothing from many of the bodies brought to Tuxtla Gutiérrez from combat areas. As a result, the CNDH scientists contended, the forensic pathologists with the federal Attorney General's office probably had no idea which of the dozens of bodies in their possession corresponded to the five bodies found in the marketplace.[93]

To set the record straight, the CNDH experts retrieved the clothing and, using press photographs from the crime scene, went from body to body until they identified the five bodies found lying next to one another in the Ocosingo marketplace. They then autopsied and photographed the bodies.

At the Commission's offices, the CNDH scientists spread out two sets of photographs on a table for Snow and Arruza. The U.S. scientists first examined the press photographs of the crime scene. One photograph clearly showed four bodies lying face down on the sidewalk next to a concrete stall, and a fifth body slightly off the curb and in the market passageway. Snow suggested that the men were probably on their knees and were shot by somebody standing within 1.5 meters or less behind them. The bodies then fell face forwards, causing the facial abrasions which were evident in the press photographs.

Looking through the autopsy photographs, Snow and Arruza noted that each of the bodies had entrance wounds, around 9 millimeters in size, to the back or the side of the head. They concluded that the wounds were caused by low-power weapons, most likely a 9-millimeter sidearm, the type of weapon carried by Mexican army officers.

---

[93] Víctor Ballinas, "Posible, que las 5 personas muertas en Ocosingo hayan sido ejecutadas," *La Jornada*, February 2, 1994, p. 10.

Madrazo ended the meeting by thanking the U.S. scientists for having confirmed the CNDH's theory: namely, that there was a high probability that the Ocosingo five had been summarily executed, and that members of the Mexican army could not be excluded as the perpetrators of these crimes. Madrazo said that he would immediately inform the PGR of these findings, and that they would be released publicly.

On several occasions the following week, the PHR representatives contacted the offices of the CNDH in San Cristóbal de las Casas to inquire about the outcome of Jorge Madrazo's meeting with the PGR, but there was no response. On January 27, PHR issued a press release and sent a letter to Madrazo urging him to release the CNDH's medicolegal findings on the Ocosingo five, "even if they contradict conclusions drawn by other agencies, governmental or otherwise."

The following day, the CNDH issued a press statement announcing that the military prosecutor, General Mario Guillermo Fromow García, had opened an investigation into the deaths of the Ocosingo five.[94] Nowhere in the statement did the CNDH mention the specific discrepancies between the findings of the PGR's forensic experts and the conclusions arrived jointly by forensic scientists affiliated with PHR and the Commission. Nor did the press bulletin mention the CNDH's conclusion, expressed to the PHR representatives a week earlier, that the Ocosingo five had been summarily executed. Instead, the bulletin referred to the "possibility" that the summary executions had taken place.

There were two other findings omitted in the press statement that had been agreed upon by the CNDH and PHR experts. One was the presence of 9-millimeter entrance wounds in the autopsy and crime scene photographs, and another was the sign of ligature marks on the wrists of the bodies. Finally, the CNDH bulletin stated that the CNDH and PGR forensic experts were in complete agreement as to the results of their separate

---

[94] *Bolétin de Prensa*, Comisión Nacional de Derechos Humanos, January 28, 1994.

autopsies, even though the Attorney General's experts had autopsied only two of the five bodies from the Ocosingo market.[95]

On February 2, PHR representative Thomas Crane met with Jorge Madrazo to discuss the press statement. Crane pressed Madrazo on the bulletin's ambiguities. Why had the CNDH been so reluctant to acknowledge that the Ocosingo five had been summarily executed? Brushing the question aside, Madrazo replied that what really mattered was that the federal Attorney General now agreed that the Ocosingo five had been executed.[96] Why then, Crane asked, hadn't the PGR released a clarification of its earlier findings? Madrazo said that it was not his business to be concerned about what the Attorney General published or didn't publish. Again, what really mattered, he explained, was that the

---

[95] The CNDH bulletin states: "As for the results of the autopsies carried out by the PGR on five corpses, which were made known by that office on January 7, 1994, there are no discrepancies with the National Commission of Human Rights, since the exact whereabouts of the Ocosingo market bodies was not possible to discover until after January 7, when the clothes they were wearing at the time of death were found; these clothes were in the possession of the Chiapas state Attorney General's office, and had not been handed over to the PGR staff. On carrying out a second autopsy of these exact bodies, there was no difference whatsoever between the findings of the CNDH and the PGR."

"En cuanto a los resultados de las necropsias practicadas por la PGR en 5 cadáveres, que fueron dados a concer por esa dependencia el 7 de enero de 1994, no existen discrepancias con la Comisión Nacional de Derechos Humanos, dado que la ubicación exacta de los cadáveres del mercado de Ocosingo no fue posible sino hasta después del 7 de enero, cuando se encontraron las ropas que vestían al ocurrir la muerte; estas ropas estaban en posesión de la Procuraduría General de Justicia del Estado de Chiapas y no habían sido entregadas al personal de la PGR. Al practicarse una segunda renecropsia en los cadáveres precisos, no existió entre los peritos de la CNDH y de la PGR diferencia alguna."

[96] See Jessica Krammerman, "Admiten equivocación en necropsia," *Reforma*, February 3, 1994.

Commission had ensured that the PGR's investigation would continue and that the military had opened its own investigation.

For the next month, none of the three government agencies investigating the Ocosingo killings released any new information. Then, on March 16, the CNDH announced that they had identified a civilian, Francisco Rodas Gómez, as one of the Ocosingo five. According to the victim's girlfriend, Margarita Sánchez Ruiz, at 2:00 pm on January 2, Rodas Gómez left his home with a friend, Alfonso Burguete Bulnes, to see what was happening in the market. Five minutes later, while crossing the market, the two men heard gunshots and ran for cover in separate directions. According to Burguete Bulnes, that was the last time he saw his friend alive.

There was no further official news on the case until April 7, when the federal Attorney General's office issued a press bulletin on new developments in the Ocosingo killings.[97] This time, according to the bulletin, the federal Attorney General's office, the military prosecutor, and the CNDH were in complete agreement on the following facts pertaining to the deaths of the Ocosingo five:

- The deaths were the result of summary executions;

- All of the bodies, as noted by the CNDH, exhibited a "coup de grace," bullet wound to the head;

- The five individuals were executed and died in the same location;

- The time of death was the same for all five individuals;

---

[97] PGR Bulletin, No. 142/94, April 7, 1994.

- The ligatures were present on the bodies before death;

- The army was not involved in the executions.

The PGR bulletin also stated that the agency had identified another civilian among the five bodies in the Ocosingo market. The individual, Pablo Santiz Gómez, lived in Oxchuc, a village located approximately twenty kilometers west of Ocosingo, where he was the owner and driver of a minibus. According to the PGR, the bus driver had been "captured by the Zapatistas on Sunday, January 2, and transferred to Ocosingo, where he appeared dead in the market, next to Rodas."[98]

Coupling this new information with their forensic findings, the PGR now placed the time of death for the Ocosingo five at between 2:00 pm and 3:00 pm on January 2, approximately forty-eight hours before the bodies were discovered. The agency went on to argue that since government troops were not present in the center of Ocosingo at the estimated time of death, the army could not be held responsible for the killings. Finally, the PGR noted that "the Mexican Army had not detained any civilians, but had assisted them whenever possible, a fact which was apparent in the testimony of Romeo Sánchez who, while riding his bicycle, had helped the army find entry roads to the town of Ocosingo."

On April 22, PHR and HRW/Americas sent a letter to federal Attorney General Diego Valadéz pointing out several contradictions and omissions of fact in the agency's bulletin and criticizing its exoneration of army personnel from any possible involvement in the killings. The first contradiction related to the

---

[98] It is worth noting that the PGR's contention that two of the Ocosingo market place victims were civilians conflicts with Marcos's view of the events given in March 1994. Marcos said "Some of our combatants were taken prisoner in Ocosingo, and were executed after being tied up.... there were about ten of our people; it was clear that all of them showed signs of having been detained previously." Interview by local human rights investigators with Subcomandante Marcos, March 1994.

PGR's claim that army troops were not present in the Ocosingo market at the time of the killings. This contention was inconsistent with several independent press reports. For example, the San Cristóbal de las Casas daily, *El Tiempo*,[99] reported that the Zapatistas entered into combat with the army in the center of Ocosingo at 3:45 pm.on January 2, while *La Jornada*[100] put the start of the battle at 3:00 pm. Furthermore, one of the witnesses cited in both the CNDH and PGR bulletins, Alfonso Burguete Bulnes, confirms that he heard gunfire near the marketplace at approximately 2:05 pm, and that the firing was sufficiently intense for him to run for cover.

Another large hole in the PGR's case is their identification of one of the Ocosingo five as Pablo Santiz Gómez. According to interviews conducted by HRW/Americas with members of his family, Santiz Gómez's relatives last saw him at his home in Oxchuc on the morning of January 2, when about thirty Zapatistas climbed aboard his minibus, along with Santiz Gómez and his son, Uber. The bus, with Uber driving, then departed. According to its license plate identification (386-HC2), this same bus was found riddled with bullets near the army base of Rancho Nuevo, located on Route 199 between San Cristóbal de las Casas and Ocosingo, with the bodies of fourteen persons, including several presumed guerrillas, lying close by. The PGR bulletin failed to note this fact.

Nor did the PGR bulletin mention that its forensic pathologists had issued death certificates for Pablo Santiz Gómez and his son, Uber, on February 23, 1994, in Tuxtla Gutiérrez, nearly seven weeks prior to the PGR bulletin (see photographs).

---

[99] *El Tiempo*, January 3, 1994.

[100] Matilde Pérez and Rosa Rojas, "Fuerte combate en Ocosingo entre soldados y el EZLN; versión de 50 alzados muertos," *La Jornada*, January 3, 1994, p. 5.

The official cause of death[101] in both cases was attributed to massive gunshot wound trauma, while the place of death was given as "the stretch of road between San Cristóbal and Oxchuc." This placed the location of the bodies in the vicinity of the Rancho Nuevo army base, and not in the Ocosingo market. Moreover, relatives have recognized the two men in autopsy photographs and in press photographs taken of the fourteen bodies lying next to the bus.

2. Eleven Deaths in or near the IMSS (Mexican Social Security Institute) Hospital in Ocosingo

On January 5, the military restricted access by journalists and human rights workers to Ocosingo and other areas formerly controlled by the EZLN. The ban lasted for seven days. On January 12, one of the first delegations to travel to Ocosingo was a team comprised of representatives from PHR, HRW/Americas, and three national human rights organizations, including the Centro de Derechos Humanos Fray Fancisco de Vitoria (CDHFFV).[102]

During a later stay in Ocosingo, the Mexican human rights workers interviewed medical staff and former patients at the IMSS hospital about reports of a mass grave in the Panteón Municipal, or municipal cemetery. The grave was said to contain the bodies

---

[101] For instance, the cause of death in the case of Pablo Santiz Gómez is given as "A consequencia de shock neurogénico y shock hipovolémico agudo segundarios a las lesiones de masa encefálica y de videra intretarcica causados por proyectil de arma de fuego." (Neurogenic and hypovolemic shock secondary to injuries of the brain and thoracic vescera caused by gunshot wounds.)

[102] See Comisión Mexicana de Defensa y Promoción de los Derechos Humanos, El Centro de Derechos Humanos Miguel Agustín Pro Juárez, A.C., Centro de Derechos Humanos Fray Francisco de Vitoria, A.C., Red Nacional de Organismos Civiles de Derechos Humanos "Todos los Derechos Para Todos," *Informe Preliminar.*

of eleven persons killed in or near the hospital during the army offensive against EZLN forces on January 3.

According to the CDHFFV, early in the afternoon of January 3, army troops had engaged a small group of Zapatistas in a shootout near the hospital. Soldiers killed two rebels and apparently entered the hospital in search of another one. At least one patient claimed soldiers entered a room and opened fire, killing or wounding two patients and eight of their relatives who had come to take them home.[103] One female patient, Rosa López Gómez, said that soldiers took away her husband, Manuel, and his brother, Mariano, who were visiting her after a caesarian section.[104]

The following day, the army closed the hospital and transferred patients to facilities in other towns or sent them home. Local residents reported that some patients, still recovering from surgery and in their hospital gowns, were found wandering the streets of Ocosingo (see Chapter VII). Meanwhile, the hospital director, Dr. S.L.C. Cordova, and his staff of twelve doctors left Ocosingo. The hospital remained closed until January 13.

On January 4, the day after the army entered the hospital, soldiers allegedly supervised the burial of eleven bodies in the municipal cemetery, located approximately one hundred meters from the hospital. The soldiers broke down a section of the

---

[103] During its visit to the hospital on January 12, the human rights delegation found a bloody stretcher in the garbage and blood stains in the room where the shooting had allegedly taken place.

[104] Doctors of the World, *Violations of Medical Neutrality During Mexican Armed Forces Occupation of Towns in Chiapas in January 1994 During the EZLN's Uprising*, February 18, 1994. Also, see Triunfo Elizalde, "Ocho torturados, 12 desapariciones y 6 ejecuciones sumarias en Chiapas," *La Jornada*, January 20, 1994, p. 16 and Bill Cormier, "Mexico peasants reportedly abused," *The Boston Globe*, January 16, 1994, p. 14.

cemetery wall closest to the hospital and had local residents bring the bodies inside and bury them in a common grave.

On January 14, a CNDH team--a Commission official, two forensic doctors, and a criminologist--arrived in Ocosingo to investigate the mass grave. Near the break in the cemetery wall, the CNDH investigators found what appeared to be "a common grave covered with a bed sheet bearing the emblem and insignia of the Instituto Mexicano del Seguro Social."[105] The following day, the CNDH team exhumed and conducted field autopsies on eleven bodies from the grave. The entire process was photographed and videotaped.

In a press bulletin issued on January 16, the CNDH reported that the "eleven bodies had been buried in the same clothes that they had been wearing at the time of death, and ten of the bodies were wearing clothing that corresponded with the type worn by most members of the Ejército Zapatista de Liberación Nacional."[106] The CNDH investigator identified one of the eleven bodies, which was apparently dressed in civilian clothes, as Caralampio Trujillo de Celis. Celis's relatives, who were present at the exhumation, said he had been accidentally shot during an exchange of gunfire between soldiers and rebels near the hospital. Local officials gave Celis's body to relatives for re-burial.

The CNDH stated in the press bulletin that "the number, characteristics, and location of the wounds indicated that the ten EZLN rebels had died in combat, and that none of the bodies had wounds consistent with summary execution or the so-called 'coup de grace.'"[107] The CNDH speculated that the presence of the hospital sheet and a catheter in one of the bodies in the grave suggested at least one of the deceased had received medical

---

[105] CNDH, *Boletín de Prensa*, San Cristóbal de las Casas, January 16, 1994.

[106] *Ibid.*

[107] *Ibid.*

attention in the hospital. The CNDH also concluded that local residents had buried the bodies, although it made no mention of whether or not army personnel had supervised the burial.

On January 21, a joint CNDH/PGR team re-exhumed the Ocosingo grave to conduct a second autopsy. This time, another body, that of Miguel Morales Méndez, was identified and turned over to relatives. The nine remaining bodies were then re-interred in the same grave.

In June 1994, the CNDH issued an update on its investigation into the Ocosingo grave. Since mid-January, CNDH investigators had located and taken testimonies from several new witnesses, including hospital staff who had fled Ocosingo after the army closed the hospital on January 4. These accounts, though often contradictory, led the CNDH to construct the following sequence of events:

> It is known that members of the Mexican military entered the Instituto Mexicano del Seguro Social at 15:30 hours on January 3. Some accounts maintain that the soldiers entered without any justification, as the clinic was neither under the control of the Ejército Zapatista de Liberación nor were any members of this group ostensibly hospitalized. Nevertheless, there are declarations that members of the EZLN had temporarily occupied the hospital. Because of this, patients and their families, nurses, hospital workers, and doctors were taken to the patio in the back of the hospital by members of the Mexican army, and were subjected to constant interrogation for several hours. That night around 150 persons slept as a group in a section of the hospital. During the following day, they were evacuated, and the facility was closed by the Mexican army.[108]

---

[108] CNDH *Informe*, May 1993-May 1994, p. 637.

The CNDH also stated that, according to the men who originally buried the bodies, eight had been recovered from inside the hospital on January 4. Of the three bodies found outside the hospital, the CNDH had identified two, Caralampio Trujillo and Miguel Morales Méndez. Of the eleven bodies, the CNDH said:

> Two were civilians who had died outside of the hospital and within the line of fire of the combatants; another five bodies belonged to relatives of patients who were with them in the hospital; two more were patients who had been hospitalized earlier; one of whom had suffered a head injury, and whose autopsy revealed that the cause of death was a gunshot wound to the thorax;[109] the other had been hospitalized since December 28, 1993 with signs of tuberculosis. An autopsy revealed that his death was caused by a gunshot wound to the thorax.[110]

The CNDH identified nine of the eleven bodies: Caralampio Trujillo Ramírez, Miguel Morales Méndez, Rafael Gómez Santiz, Jacinto Gómez López, Agustín López Gómez, Mariano Gómez López, Manuel Gómez López, Baltazar Hernández Jiménez, and Francisco Hernández Jiménez. It also called on the federal Attorney General's office and the Military Prosecutor's office "to determine the manner, time, and place in which these eleven persons died, and to identify those presumably responsible for these crimes."

---

[109] This victim's name was Rafael Gómez Santiz. His neighbor, Armando Trujillo, told HRW/Americas on February 13 that Gómez had become very drunk during the New Year's celebrations and was found injured in the street, apparently after falling over and hitting his head. Rafael's brother Jacinto took him to the hospital where he was put on an intravenous drip and kept under observation. Jacinto, who was looking after his brother when the army entered the hospital, is among those listed as dead by the CNDH.

[110] *Ibid.*

Several troubling questions and issues remain regarding the Mexican government's investigation of the eleven bodies in the Ocosingo grave. To begin with, why did the PGR and CNDH perform hasty autopsies at the gravesite rather than in proper facilities with access to X-ray machines? It is also unclear whether a thorough crime scene investigation was ever conducted inside the hospital. CNDH president Jorge Madrazo and several of his investigators told PHR in April 1994 that between the first autopsy on January 15 and the second on January 21, construction workers had repaired--including re-plastering the walls--much of the damage in the hospital. Why did the authorities allow such repairs to take place? At a minimum, certain critical areas in the hospital should have been secured for a detailed forensic examination. Investigators, for instance, could have attempted to reconstruct the location of those killed within the hospital, by determining the trajectory of bullets which struck the walls, floors, and other objects. Such information, coupled with witness statements regarding the location and position of those who were allegedly shot could help determine where the shots originated from. Such information, coupled with witness statements, could help determine whether the fatal gunshots had originated from inside or outside the hospital.

Another troubling aspect of the government's investigation is the CNDH's conclusion, in its press bulletin of January 16, that ten of the eleven individuals exhumed from the mass grave were Zapatistas, a finding based solely on the clothing found on the bodies. In June 1994, however, the CNDH announced that at least nine of the eleven were civilians. The CNDH may have an explanation for this discrepancy, but it has, so far, chosen not to make it public.

Finally, there is the testimony of Rosa López Gómez, the patient who said her husband, Manuel, and his brother, Mariano, were taken away from the hospital by government soldiers. CNDH forensic scientists have identified the two men among the eleven bodies found in the common grave. Given this fact, why has the CNDH chosen not to make public the testimony of Rosa López Gómez? Circumstantial evidence suggests that army troops may be responsible for the deaths of several of the civilians found in the common grave.

3. The Cases of Severiano Santiz Gómez Sebastián Santiz López, Hermelindo Santiz Gómez[111]

Early in the morning on January 7, 1994, army troops, allegedly acting on a tip-off that Zapatistas were in the area, surrounded the ejido of Morelia, a Tzeltal village located eight kilometers east of Altamirano.[112] As helicopters circled overhead, hundreds of soldiers, accompanied by tanks and armored vehicles, entered the village. Soldiers broke into houses, stealing valuables, and detaining all the men and boys over the age of fifteen. They also ransacked the village hospital and dispensary (see Chapter VII).

The soldiers brought the men to a basketball court, which serves as Morelia's central square, and forced them to lie face down on the pavement. They were ordered to remain still and to keep their hands over their heads. If anyone moved, they were kicked or beaten with rifle butts. The men stayed there for nearly ten hours.

Humberto Santiz López, a 32-year-old farmer, told PHR/HRW that he was in a group that was forced to lie down on the floor of the small village church which faces onto the basketball court. From where he was lying, López could see everything that was going on. He recalls hearing women shouting to the soldiers to let them bring food and water to their husbands and sons. But the soldiers kept the women away at gunpoint.

---

[111] Severiano Santiz Gómez and Hermelindo Santiz Gómez are not related to Pablo Santiz Gómez.

[112] Despite published news accounts and unanimous, consistent testimonies by villagers as to the date of the army action, the Secretary of Defense issued a press bulletin on February 13, 1994, stating that the army had entered the village a day earlier, on January 6, 1994.

According to López, the leader of the army detachment, a captain, took out a list and began calling out names. He first called out the name of a 60-year-old farmer, Severiano Santiz Gómez. "When no one responded," López says, "one of our school teachers who had accompanied the soldiers to the ejido stepped forward and pointed to Severiano, saying, 'There he is, he's the one, the one in the yellow pullover.'"

Soldiers dragged Severiano Santiz Gómez into the small sacristy attached to the church. "All of us could hear the screams as they tortured him," says López. "From where I was lying, I couldn't see into the sacristy, but I saw the condition he was in afterwards. His face had been cut up so badly it looked like a sieve, and one ear was cut off. They had also broken his wrists. . .all the while, [the soldiers] kept asking him where his weapon was and to admit he was a Zapatista."[113]

Next, the army captain called out the names of Humberto's father, Sebastián Santiz López (aged 65), and Hermelindo Santiz Gómez (aged 45), as well as those of thirty-two other men. Villagers told HRW/Americas and PHR that soldiers took Sebastián to his shop directly across from the basketball court and forced him to unlock the door. The soldiers ransacked the shop, stealing money and other goods, including machetes, trousers, knives, hatchets, and soap. They also looted the government-run Conasupo store which also fronts onto the basketball court.

Sebastián and Hermelindo were eventually taken to the sacristy and interrogated under torture.[114] In the meantime, the other detainees were divided into two groups. One group was flown by helicopter to Cerro Hueco prison in Tuxtla Gutiérrez,

---

[113] According to Severiano Santiz Gómez's wife and son, electric light cables were also attached to him, electric current was applied, and his head was submerged in a bucket of water.

[114] Sebastián Santiz López's wife, Petrona López, says her husband was beaten in her presence.

and another was loaded onto trucks and taken to the town of Comitán before being transferred to Cerro Hueco. Several detainees later charged that they had been tortured en route to Comitán.[115]

At approximately 6:00 pm that evening, the soldiers left Morelia and headed in the direction of Altamirano. As they departed, villagers watched a green armored personnel carrier, bearing a red cross, pull up to the basketball court. Using stretchers, soldiers loaded Severiano Santiz Gómez, Sebastián Santiz López, and Hermelindo Santiz Gómez, who were bleeding heavily, into the vehicle and drove away. The army captain told the wives of the three men that they would be taken to a hospital for treatment.

For the next five weeks, the widows of the three men searched in vain for their husbands. Sebastián's wife, Petrona López, visited hospitals in Altamirano and Ocosingo. But Sebastián had never been admitted. Finally, she filed a complaint with the Ministro Público and the National Commission of Human Rights.

The first news of the fate of the three men reached Morelia on the afternoon of February 10. Earlier in the day, peasants who were cutting wood near the dirt road linking Morelia and Altamirano had come across what appeared to be scraps of clothing and human remains. The site was about 300 meters from a former army checkpoint. Bypassing the local authorities, the village leaders sent a confidential message of the discovery to the Fray Bartolomé de las Casas Center for Human Rights in San Cristóbal.[116]

---

[115] See Raúl Monge, "Testimonios implacables: el Ejército responsable de la detención, desaparición y muerte de los tres indígenas del ejido Morelia," *Proceso*, February 21, 1994, pp. 24-31.

[116] Representatives of the Morelia ejido later told HRW/PHR that they had called on the assistance of nongovernmental organizations because of their distrust of the Mexican government.

On the morning of February 11, the Center's director, Pablo Romo, travelled to Morelia, accompanied by PHR representative Thomas Crane and HRW/Americas researcher Sebastian Brett. Before leaving San Cristóbal, Dr. Crane notified the local CNDH office of the purpose of their trip.

Villagers met the delegation on the Altamirano road and led them down a sloping pasture to a wooded embankment. Searching in the underbrush, the delegation found bones and remnants of clothing scattered over an area approximately the size of a tennis court. Villagers recognized boots and articles of clothing belonging to the missing men. Among the skeletonized remains were partial and complete mandibles; one of these had prominent silver dental work. Sebastián's son, Humberto, identified the dental work and an intact upper dental plate found at the site as belonging to his father. The PHR-HRW/Americas representatives cordoned off the area to establish a crime scene, and photographed and recorded the location of the bones and clothing.

Soon thereafter, officials from the CNDH and the state Attorney General's office arrived and took control of the crime scene. While the investigators photographed the remains and clothing and placed them in three gunny sacks, reporters and onlookers wandered freely within the protective cordon. Before leaving, the official in charge, Luis Eusebio Mancilla Trujillo, signed an agreement with the ejido leaders stating that his office would transport the evidence to Tuxtla Gutiérrez for forensic examination and return it to the village within 72 hours.

The government officials then left for the state capital. An hour later, however, soldiers at the army checkpoint in Altamirano seized the three bags of evidence. (The army later claimed that the evidence was seized because the government officials did not have the proper licenses for the transport of human remains.) Later that day, the bags were deposited in the Altamirano municipal office.

On February 12, a reporter who had been present at the site of the discovery the day before, received a telephone call from Luis Eusebio Mancilla Trujillo, the PGJ official in charge of the investigation. Mancilla Trujillo told the reporter that the state Attorney General's office was now finished with the bones, which had never gotten beyond Altamirano. He asked if the reporter would return the remains to Morelia.

When Dr. Crane learned of the conversation the next morning, he promptly called Mancilla. Under prolonged questioning, Mancilla now told a different story. The remains, he said, had in fact been examined by forensic specialists in Tuxtla Gutiérrez and were now en route back to Altamirano for delivery to the ejido. Alarmed by the discrepancies in these two accounts, Dr. Crane, along with members of a local human rights group and several reporters, quickly left for Altamirano.

The delegation went first to the Altamirano Municipal Office, where they spoke with an official of the Public Ministry, Iris Velazco Ruiz, and the mayor, Arnulfo Cruz Decelis. The town officials said that the remains had never left Altamirano, and denied that the state Attorney General's office had ever forensically examined the evidence. In fact, the mayor said, the remains were being examined in the very building where they were sitting. Dr. Crane insisted that he be present at the examination, and was taken to a patio in the building. There, he found fifteen armed soldiers, some wearing surgical gloves, busily jotting down notes as they weighed and photographed the confiscated bones and clothing. They turned out to be a team of military forensic specialists flown in from Mexico City. Although the soldiers refused to be interviewed, two officers--José Luis Ramírez Negrete and Juan Bolaños--commented that the bones were from men in their twenties and that they had been dead at least three years. Another officer said they were examining the remains because of accusations that the army was responsible for the deaths of the three men.

When Dr. Crane suggested that the military's intervention in a civilian criminal investigation was illegal under Mexican law, an army attorney, Francisco Vasquez Rana, claimed that the municipality had invited the military experts to examine the remains. He produced a letter from the army to the Public Ministry requesting permission to examine the evidence. The letter bore a ministerial seal and the word "received" was written in Spanish next to it, but there was no indication that the ministry had actually granted the army permission. Clearly exasperated, the army lawyer insisted that a ministry official had given him verbal permission to proceed with the examination. However, in an earlier interview with Dr. Crane, the ministry official and the mayor had denied giving anyone permission to examine the evidence.[117]

Dr. Crane and the other members of the delegation stayed that night at a guest house owned by the San Carlos Hospital. The hospital, run by the Sisters of Charity of the Saint Vincent de Paul Society, provides free medical care to the poor and has long been a target of threats from local cattle ranchers and businessmen, who claim that the nuns and staff are Zapatista sympathizers (see Chapter VII). For years, and especially since the January uprising, municipal authorities and town caciques have organized demonstrations in front of the hospital, demanding that the nuns leave.

Walking through the town square that evening, Dr. Crane was surrounded by about 200 men who looked menacingly at him but eventually allowed him to pass. Early the next morning, Dr. Crane stood by the hospital gate and watched soldiers run back and forth in the front of the hospital, yelling, "We are the messengers of death!" and "Death to the Zapatistas!" When the officer in charge noticed the doctor, he shouted insults and photographed him.

---

[117] An army surgeon, Dr. Negrete, who had been in Altamirano since the early days of the conflict, reportedly told a CONPAZ observer that the purpose of the examination was to help the army prepare its defense should criminal charges ever be brought against it.

By late morning, several local and army officials had gathered at the mayor's office to decide what to do with the Morelia remains. Among them was a representative from the state Attorney General's Office, Miguel Angel Esquinca, who had brought along several heavily-armed guards. He told the gathering that he was there to return the bones to the ejido. When Dr. Crane asked Esquinca why his office wasn't going to perform a complete forensic examination, the official refused to answer his question. Esquinca placed the three sacks in a large wooden box and, along with several CNDH representatives, left for Morelia.

The government officials found an angry crowd waiting for them in Morelia. As the press and human rights advocates watched, the village leaders forced Esquinca to acknowledge in a signed statement that the army had illegally seized the bones and clothing. He also acknowledged in the statement that the remains were those of Sebastián Santiz López, Severiano Santiz Gómez, and Hermalindo Santiz Gómez. After signing and fingerprinting the document, the village leaders insisted that the government official help carry the box of bones and clothing into the church.

After Esquinca left, Dr. Crane met with the ejido leaders to discuss the possibility of having forensic anthropologist Clyde Snow examine the remains. They agreed. Dr. Crane then opened the box of evidence, carefully separated the bones from the wet clothing, and laid them out to dry. (Several days later, villagers discovered more bones in the ravine, including a cranium and several long bones and ribs that had been overlooked during the search of the ravine. These remains were also deposited in the wooden box.)

On February 17, 1994, a CNDH forensic team travelled to Morelia to examine the bones. The scientists presented a sealed letter to the ejido leaders signed by Dr. Thomas Crane and Roger Maldonado of CONPAZ. In the letter, Crane and Maldonado said that they supported the CNDH's forensic investigation and called on the villagers to cooperate with the government scientists.[118] But the ejido leaders refused, saying that the remains could only be examined in the presence of an independent forensic scientist.

A week later, Dr. Crane returned to Morelia, this time with PHR Senior Forensic Consultant, Clyde Snow and two CNDH forensic medical specialists, Dr. Margarita Franco Luna and Dr. Epifano Salazar Araiza, and two CNDH criminologists, Sergio Cirnes Zuñiga, and Alfredo Carrillo García. Villagers cleaned out the ransacked clinic and set up several tables for the investigators, who spent the next two days poring over the remains.

In most medicolegal investigations of skeletal remains, the forensic anthropologist sets out to establish the identity of the deceased and to determine the time, cause, and manner of death. Antemortem dental or medical X-rays often provide the most immediate means of identifying skeletal remains. However, if sufficient radiological evidence is not available, the forensic anthropologist will undertake an anthropological study of the skeleton. Such a study involves determining the skeleton's age at death, sex, race, stature, and handedness. This information is compared with the deceased's antemortem characteristics to see if they match. Similarly, old diseases and injuries often leave their traces on the skeleton, providing evidence for positive identification.

---

[118] The text of the letter, translated from Spanish, reads as follows: "Friends of Morelia: Our co-worker Edith informed us today that the National Commission of Human Rights will go to Morelia tomorrow to examine the remains of Severiano, Sebastián, and Hermelindo. We believe that civilian investigations can be useful for documenting the truth. If you decide to let [the CNDH] study the evidence, you have the right to be present during the entire examination. We support the intention of the National Commission of Human Rights to conduct this examination. You also have the right to receive a copy of all that is done. As we had agreed, Physicians for Human Rights--the friends of Tom--are still planning to come, although we do not know exactly when. Warm regards, Dr. Thomas Crane and Roger Maldonado."

91

Through a combination of training and experience, forensic anthropologists are able to distinguish between various types of trauma to the bone which the inexperienced eye may fail to detect. Signs of violent death on the skeleton vary from the grossly obvious, such as massive blunt force trauma or bullet holes in the skull, to easily overlooked minor cuts or nicks by a fatal stab wound. Even strangulation can leave its mark on the bone: ligature or manual strangulation often result in the fracture of the hyoid bone, a small and delicate U-shaped bone located at the root of the tongue, which is seldom recovered unless the grave is carefully excavated.

During the first day of the forensic investigation, Dr. Snow inventoried the bones and began reconstructing the skulls. Meanwhile, Dr. Crane interviewed relatives of the missing men to obtain antemortem data to help in skeletal identification. Before leaving Morelia that evening, the investigators arranged for the room to be secured and guarded for the night. In accordance with local custom, one of the village's religious leaders placed votive candles next to the skulls where they burned throughout the night.

Sorting through the Morelia remains the following day, Snow found that animal scavengers had badly damaged most of the bones. Even so, he managed to attribute to different people several sets of bones and bone fragments (see Appendix A). Snow determined that the remains belonged to three American Indian males who were between forty to seventy years of age at the time of death. Based on the condition of the bones, he placed the time of death at a few weeks to a few months prior to his examination. Several perimortem fractures on the three skulls suggested that sometime around the time of death the men had been hit with hard objects such as rifle butts or clubs.

Snow concluded that the skeletal findings appeared to be consistent with the antemortem descriptions of Severiano Santiz Gómez, Hermelindo Santiz Gómez, and Sebastián Santiz López. But without more specific evidence, such as antemortem X-rays, to compare to the remains, he was hesitant to make a positive identification at that time.

92

Given the condition of the remains and the lack of antemortem X-rays, the most promising means of identifying the remains with scientific certainty was through DNA "fingerprinting."

Deoxyribonucleic acid (DNA) is the chromosomal material that carries genes, the blueprints of every organism. Within the three billion chemical units of a person's entire set of chromosomes lie features unique to each individual. By the same token, some of these features are common only to members of the same family, and are handed down generation by generation.

In forensics, DNA is extracted from body fluids, tissue, or even bone fragments and teeth at a crime scene. The molecular features that vary among individuals are located and reproduced in a laboratory on an autoradiograph, a print much like an X-ray. These variable "polymorphisms" show up as a row of blotches irregularly spaced in a vertical lane. These "bands" look something like a bar code used to mark goods in a supermarket. If a suspect in a crime had been apprehended, a similar autoradiograph can be made from his or her DNA, and the two prints compared. If the bands match, the DNA at the crime scene belongs to the suspect. The method, while not infallible, is highly reliable.

After consulting with the village leaders, Snow extracted a tooth from each of the skulls for DNA testing. Later, in March, Dr. Crane collected blood samples from several maternal relatives of the deceased for comparison with the DNA extracted from the teeth. Both the teeth and the blood samples were sent to Mary-Claire King, Ph.D., a renowned geneticist at the University of California, Berkeley.

Since the mid-1980s, Dr. King had worked with Argentine geneticists to determine the biological identities of dozens of children who had disappeared during military rule in Argentina in the 1970s and were later adopted by military families.[119] In recent years, Dr. King and her colleagues had begun applying mitochondrial DNA (mtDNA) analysis to identify the skeletal remains of the disappeared. This forensic method is particularly useful when antemortem records are nonexistent or skeletal remains are too fragmentary.[120] The method requires comparing mtDNA extracted from the teeth or bone of the deceased with mtDNA obtained from blood samples or hair follicles from maternal relatives.[121] If the samples match, it is considered a positive identification.

While Snow was fairly sure the fracture lines on the three skulls were the result of blunt force trauma, he still wanted to X-ray them for bullet fragments. On the afternoon of the second and last day of the forensic examination, Snow and Crane, along with the CNDH scientists, left Morelia with the three reconstructed skulls bound for the IMSS hospital in Ocosingo. They passed through the army checkpoint at Altamirano and proceeded to Ocosingo. At the hospital, a radiologic examination of the skulls showed no evidence of small metallic fragments characteristic of gunshot injury.

---

[119] See Anna María Di Londardo, Pierre Darlu, Max Baur, et al., "Human Genetics and Human Rights: Identifying the Families of Kidnapped Children," *American Journal of Forensic Medicine and Pathology, 1984*; 5:339-347.

[120] mtDNA analysis has several features that make it attractive in cases where there is little or no antemortem information on the deceased. Unlike chromosomal DNA, which is inherited from both parents, both male and female children inherit mtDNA only from their mother. Therefore, when using mtDNA analysis, a DNA sample from only one maternal relative is required to identify the victim. That individual might be the victim's mother, a sibling, maternal grandmother, or maternal aunt or uncle. mtDNA analysis is particularly valuable in situations where one or both parents are deceased or cannot be located.

[121] See Charles Ginter, Laurie Issel-Tarver, Mary-Claire King. Identifying individuals by sequencing mitochondrial DNA from teeth. *Nature*, 1992; 2:135-138.

Having completed their forensic investigation, Snow and Crane returned to San Cristóbal that evening. In the meantime, the CNDH scientists set out to return the skulls to the residents of Morelia. At about midnight they reached the army checkpoint in Altamirano, where soldiers seized the remains and detained and questioned the CNDH scientists for nearly five hours. Later that day, the military re-assembled their forensic specialists to examine the recently reconstructed skulls. Even the on-site intervention of CNDH president Jorge Madrazo failed to prevent this apparently illegal forensic examination. When local human rights workers urged Madrazo to appeal to his superiors to prevent this illegal military usurpation of civilian rule, he replied that it was better to put up with violations of constitutional guarantees than risk incurring a state of exception when all rights are summarily suspended.

The remains were finally returned to Morelia by Roger Maldonado of CONPAZ who slipped out a back door of the Public Ministry while angry pro-army demonstrators threatened the human rights workers in front of the building.

On February 27, the people of Morelia buried the remains in the village cemetery.

By late-September 1994, Dr. Snow had completed his final report on the Morelia remains (see Appendix A). He concluded:

> These human remains, which were recovered from
> a ravine near Morelia, Chiapas, are those of three
> indigenous males who died from multiple blunt
> force trauma one to three months prior to the
> discovery of the remains on February 10, 1994.
> The remains are generally consistent with
> Hermelindo Santiz Gómez, Severiano Santiz
> Gómez, and Sebastián Santiz López.

Meanwhile, Dr. Mary-Claire King and her colleagues at the University of California at Berkeley had obtained preliminary findings on the teeth taken from the three skulls and the blood samples from the maternal relatives of the three missing men. While final analyses still need to be completed, the geneticists had positively identified the remains of Severiano Santiz Gómez and Hermelindo Santiz Gómez based on mtDNA sequencing (see Appendix B). However, the analysis of teeth obtained from the third individual--believed to be Sebastián Santiz López--and blood samples from his maternal relatives had not been completed.

Based on the anthropological and preliminary genetic findings, PHR and Human Rights Watch/Americas conclude that *prima facie* evidence exists to charge Mexican army personnel in the detention, torture, and murder of Hermelindo Santiz Gómez, Severiano Santiz Gómez, and Sebastián Santiz López who were last seen alive in army custody in the ejido of Morelia on January 7, 1994.

4. Two Murders in Las Margaritas

Las Margaritas was one of four towns occupied by the Zapatistas on the night of December 31. The rebels commandeered several civilian vehicles as they approached the town. Among them was a cattle truck driven by a 21-year-old man named Jorge Mariano Solís. The man reportedly gave up the vehicle without struggle and was left by the roadside unharmed.

By the evening of January 2, the Zapatistas had retreated from Las Margaritas. Soon thereafter, army troops occupied the town and have remained there ever since.

At approximately 6:30 pm on January 16, military and police personnel conducted a sweep through the central square of the town and, in the presence of several witnesses, arrested Jorge Mariano Solís and Eduardo Gómez Hernández, a driver with a local peasant organization who, like Solís, had allegedly failed to resist the Zapatistas when they occupied the town.

Witnesses say that the two men were taken to the Las Margaritas police station. A friend of Solís's father, Evandro

Gómez Cruz, says he saw his friend's son, Jorge, sitting in a chair next to another young man in the police station at about 7:00 pm that evening. Shortly thereafter, Cruz went to see Jorge's father.

Other witnesses claim that at approximately 7:30 pm soldiers loaded Jorge Mariano Solís and Eduardo Gómez Hernández into a military vehicle and drove away. It was the last time either man was seen alive. The following day, Solís's father and mother, together with Hernández's father, went to the jail to look for their sons. The authorities denied that either man had been detained there. The parents then went to the mayor who denied any knowledge of their whereabouts.

On January 24, a man hunting rabbits discovered the bodies of two young men near a dirt road about eight kilometers north of Las Margaritas. Having heard of the recent disappearances of Solís and Hernández, the hunter went directly to their families and brought them to the site. Once the relatives identified the two men, they informed the local authorities who came to the crime scene and transported the bodies to Las Margaritas. Although only a gross examination was performed, the official cause of death was given as multiple gunshot wounds.

PHR became involved in the case on January 25, the day after the discovery of the corpses. By then, the state Attorney General, who was dissatisfied with the way matters had been handled in Las Margaritas, had transferred the bodies to a hospital in Comitán so that proper autopsies could be performed. Meanwhile, the CNDH had invited PHR representatives Clyde Snow and Thomas Crane to observe the postmortems, along with several CNDH investigators.

Crane recalled the scene as the group waited outside the hospital in Comitán:

> We arrived at the hospital, and there were family
> members of the deceased waiting outside. The
> CNDH investigators began conducting interviews
> right there in the parking lot within earshot of

rifle-carrying federal police with their SWAT T-shirts and dozens of onlookers who were waiting at a bus stop, and even with a drunk weaving in among the interviewees. They asked only the most basic questions, and made no attempt to conduct confidential interviews.

Inside the hospital morgue, the group observed the autopsy while a CNDH investigator videotaped and photographed the process. The state pathologist concluded that both men had died as a result of multiple stab wounds to the upper torso. There was no clearcut physical evidence that the two men had been tortured before they were stabbed to death. However, signs of torture could have been absent or difficult to detect because the bodies were in an advanced state of petrification and had been badly scavenged by animals while lying in the open. Snow and Crane, as well as several CNDH forensic scientists who later reviewed the photographs and video of the autopsies, felt that the pathologist who performed the autopsies was sloppy and substandard in his work, but they concurred with his findings.

Late in the afternoon following the autopsies, Snow and Crane visited the crime scene. They located the depressions where the bodies had been found and began searching in the underbrush for any possible clues left behind by the local investigators. Within minutes, Crane had found a shirt button near one of the depressions. Snow, meanwhile, began walking along a footpath toward the road. He had gone no more than forty feet when he looked to one side of the path. There, resting in the grass, was what appeared to be a plastic card. He picked up the object and flipped it over. On the top of the card it read, in Spanish: "Voter Identification Card," and below that was a portrait photograph of Eduardo Gómez Hernández.

The circumstantial and physical evidence points to the involvement of police and military personnel in the murders of Jorge Mariano Solís and Eduardo Gómez Hernández. However, at the time of writing, October 1994, no one has been charged with these crimes.

VII. VIOLATIONS OF MEDICAL NEUTRALITY

The Geneva Conventions of 1949 and Protocol II,[122] to which Mexico is a party, describe the rights of the wounded and sick in times of noninternational armed conflict to receive medical care "to the fullest extent practicable and with the least possible delay."[123] They also call for all sides in a conflict to respect and protect medical personnel in the performance of their medical duties compatible with medical ethics "regardless of the persons benefitting therefrom."[124] Violations of medical neutrality can include firing upon hospitals and clinics; interference in the delivery of health care; establishing a military presence within a hospital, thus intimidating health workers and patients alike; and direct assaults or threats against health personnel.[125]

Delivery of Health Care

Following more than sixty relatively peaceful years, the New Year's Day rebellion caught civilian, military, and police authorities in Chiapas by complete surprise. Unused to armed conflict, Mexico's civilian and military medical personnel had never delivered health care in a conflict zone.

---

[122] See Committee on Foreign Affairs, U.S. House of Representatives, "The Geneva Conventions of 1949," "Common Article 3," and "Protocol Additional to the Geneva Conventions of 12 August 1949, and Relating to the Protection of Victims of Non-International Armed Conflicts" (Protocol II), In: *Human Rights Documents: Compilation of Documents Pertaining to Human Rights* (Washington, D.C.: Government Printing Office, 1983), pp. 547-559.

[123] *Ibid.*, Protocol II, Part III, p. 553.

[124] *Ibid.*, Protocol II, Part III, Article 10, p. 554.

[125] See Alma Baccino-Astrada, *Manual on the Rights and Duties of Medical Personnel in Armed Conflict* (Geneva: International Committee of the Red Cross and The League of Red Cross Societies, 1982).

During the rebellion and its aftermath, scores of health care workers fled, leaving behind poorly trained health promoters and scant supplies. Cases of cholera and chicken pox began to rise, adding to the endemic burden of respiratory and diarrheal disease. Chlorination teams from San Cristóbal could no longer travel to villages to chlorinate wells to prevent the spread of parasitic and bacterial diseases. Immunization programs for residents in rebel-held areas also ceased entirely, either because of lack of funds or because the government cut off health services to punish the Zapatistas and their presumed sympathizers.

For most of the state's residents, access to health care is a luxury even in peacetime.[126] Often those in greatest need live in remote areas where living conditions foster illness and disease. Running water, which helps promote good health, is available in only fifty-eight percent of households, versus a national rate of eighty percent. In 1990, Chiapas recorded the highest number of new cases of malaria and had the third highest rate of tuberculosis in the country. Trachoma, a major and easily preventable cause of blindness in newborns, is also highly prevalent in Chiapas, where fifty percent of Mexico's new cases originate. Diarrheal diseases cause death in Chiapas at three times the national rate. Mortality from measles is 31 per 100,000, four times the national rate. Chiapas ranks fourth from the bottom of Mexico's thirty-one states in life expectancy.

San Carlos Hospital in Altamirano

Among the medical establishments hardest hit in the wake of the January uprising was the San Carlos Hospital in the town of Altamirano.[127] Founded in 1969 by the Sisters of Charity of

---

[126] See Secretaría de Educación, Cultura y Salud de Chiapas, "La Salud de Chiapas, Su Magnitud y Transendencia," 1993. All data is from 1990.

[127] This account of events at San Carlos Hospital is based on interviews with several staff members by PHR representatives between January and March 1994.

the Saint Vincent de Paul Society, the hospital maintains a fifty-six bed in-patient facility, as well as ambitious outpatient programs in primary health, vaccinations, and dental care. The hospital is so popular that even after the rebellion began, patients bypassed government facilities to come to the clinic from more than a hundred miles away.

Because of their explicit mission to care for the poor and indigenous people of the area, the nuns who operate the hospital and clinics have frequently run afoul of Altamirano's political authorities, who are mostly cattle ranchers and PRI loyalists. Over the years, the hospital's most outspoken opponent has been Jorge Constantino Kanter, who is both president of the local cattle ranchers association and the local PRI. Ranchers and their kin have long resented having to seek medical attention at the hospital, where they must wait in line, without preferential treatment, next to indigenous laborers and their families. This resentment, coupled with the opinion held by many ranchers that those who provide social services to impoverished indigenous communities must be subversive, led to a growing number of attacks on the hospital by the local newspaper and radio station.

On January 1, 1994, the Zapatistas took control of Altamirano after brief skirmishes with the town's police force. There were casualties on both sides, and the survivors were transported to the San Carlos hospital for care. Sister Patricia Moysen, head administrator of the hospital, later told PHR that her staff treated the wounded of both sides, in keeping with their ethical duty to care for all those placed hors de combat. Seven patients--four of them Zapatistas and the rest police--were placed in beds next to one another. According to Sister Patricia, one Zapatista soldier died of a head wound while in the hospital and one public security officer succumbed to neck injuries.

Late in the evening of January 1, a rebel commander and three guerrilla soldiers, armed with fake rifles carved from tree limbs, arrived at the hospital to supervise the facility. They stayed for almost three days, arriving at dawn, and leaving before sunset each day. Sister Patricia and the staff of the hospital report

101

that despite this occupation, the hospital was allowed to operate normally and that care for all patients proceeded without interruption or interference. The Zapatistas did commandeer the hospital truck, but left it behind when they withdrew.

When asked why the hospital staff allowed armed insurgent troops to occupy the premises in contravention of the rules of war, Sister Patricia replied that the Sisters were inexperienced in such matters, and concerned themselves primarily with the welfare of their patients, both guerrillas and police. "We saw [the rebels] were armed with only stick guns," she said. "I know nobody should enter [a hospital] armed, but whenever the police had entered, they had come with guns, and often they were drawn...And when the army came to the hospital, they came armed, too."

On the afternoon of January 5, while the Zapatista soldiers prepared to decamp from Altamirano, the rebel commander explained to the hospital staff that they would be taking their wounded as they withdrew from the town. At this time, two public security police remained hospitalized. According to Sister Patricia, the rebel commander explained that their own soldiers (one critically injured) would be shot if they left them behind. The wounded police, however, were left behind because, as the rebels explained, they had no facilities for their care. Thirty-six hours after the rebel retreat, army troops secured the town of Altamirano without incident.

The Zapatista retreat allowed PRI officials, with support of the Army, to quickly re-establish political and military control over Altamirano. Because the municipal building had been virtually destroyed by the Zapatistas, new government headquarters were set up in the town square. Immediately, a concerted campaign to intimidate and harass the nuns and the medical staff at San Carlos Hospital began. The Army arrested a laboratory technician, Juan Diego Hernández, and held him for nine days. During this time, he was reportedly tortured as his interrogators repeatedly demanded that he disclose whether the hospital contained a secret Zapatista arms cache. Diego later told

National Public Radio reporter John Burnett that his captors told him that the hospital was full of guerrillas and that he would be killed if he returned to work. After his release, Diego was examined by hospital physicians who found blood in his urine (hematuria) and multiple contusions consistent with his torture account.[128] By March 1994, three months after his detention, Diego still had no feeling in his left hand as a result of his torture.

Staff physicians at the hospital were also subjected to intimidation, threats, and ostracism of their families by the army and the PRI town hierarchy. Of the five full-time physicians, four either quit or left the hospital in the three weeks following the New Year's Day rebellion, according to Sister Patricia. Villagers in outlying communities were told that the hospital was closed. Those indigenous peasants who persevered and brought their ill family members to the hospital feared being identified as Zapatistas. The remaining doctor resisted several urgent pleas by military messengers to leave the hospital compound to evaluate sick soldiers at the military headquarters in town. He grew suspicious when the military doctor who requested his help repeatedly refused to bring his patients to the hospital where diagnostic equipment was readily available. Once, according to hospital staff, an emergency request came for the sole staff physician to attend to the wife of the military commander. In each of these cases, the army officers declined to bring their patients to the hospital. The doctor, who requests anonymity, and the nuns of the hospital are convinced that the calls for help were nothing more than ruses to lure the last doctor at San Carlos away in order to arrest him, thus crippling the institution's medical mission.

Starting in mid-January, the hospital was subjected to almost daily demonstrations denouncing the nuns as Zapatista sympathizers and calling for their expulsion from the town. The crowds that gathered at the hospital gates were directed by the local PRI president, Jorge Constantino Kanter, who publicly

---

[128] Ironically, prior to his detention, Juan Diego Hernández, a Tzeltal indian, had donated blood to help save the life of a wounded policeman.

defended his actions by claiming he had proof that the Catholic sisters had actively conspired with the rebels and that the hospital still maintained a large cache of Zapatista weapons. Although Kanter repeatedly claimed to possess a tape recording of the Dominican priests of the Ocosingo diocese discussing guerrilla tactics over shortwave radio with the rebels, he never produced the tape for journalists nor any other evidence to support his claim. As time wore on, the tenor of the almost nightly demonstrations grew more hostile. Often wives of the soldiers and women PRI functionaries appeared in the front lines of the demonstrators that converged at the hospital.

On the night of February 20, a group of women appeared in front of the hospital. This time, the demonstrators, some of whom were apparently drunk, crashed through the gates and poured into the courtyard of the hospital, physically accosting the nuns and threatening the families of patients. The demonstrators demanded that the nuns close the hospital. According to David Levinson,[129] a U.S. physician who was present at the demonstration, the leaders of the demonstration told the nuns that, "in the interests of patient safety," the staff would have until noon the next day to empty and close the facility. If they refused, the hospital would be burned to the ground.

Early the next morning, a PHR representative and several local human rights activists arrived at the hospital, followed by national and international reporters. The threatened expulsion never occurred. However, when the PHR representative walked into the center of town with two journalists to interview refugees in the emergency shelter, they were immediately surrounded and shoved by an angry crowd that quickly swelled to more than one hundred people. The leaders of the group denounced the reporters for printing lies about Altamirano. They also said that the hospital would have been torched the previous evening had there been no

---

[129] Dr. Levinson is one of several foreign physicians who have served at the San Carlos Hospital on behalf of Doctors of the World over the past twelve months. They have provided much needed medical care and a certain degree of protection for the hospital staff and patients.

reporters at the hospital. Ironically, the only "reporter" present
was probably Dr. Levinson, who photographed the demonstrators
as they swept into the hospital grounds.

Three nights later, another demonstration took place in
front of the hospital's main gates. Nuns and staff nervously
readied fire extinguishers as a man circulated through the mob
carrying a bottle filled with clear liquid and stuffed with a rag.
Less than an hour later, the garage of a prominent hospital
supporter's home was burned to the ground as police and state
judicial police looked on.

As of September 1994, harassment of the hospital
continues. Most recently, two international health care workers
recruited by Doctors of the World to work at the hospital were
given ten days to leave the country by immigration officials.
Henceforth, all foreign volunteer workers, even those providing
humanitarian aid must secure business visas, which are difficult to
obtain, to remain in the country. This new requirement appears
designed to rid the area of foreign observers.

Supplies to the San Carlos Hospital and outlying
communities suspected of harboring rebel sympathizers have also
been subject to seizure and delay. Donated food, medicine, and
supplies bound for the hospital have been impounded for hours at
the military roadblock leading into Altamirano while soldiers
search large truckloads. These same boxes are again searched
every time the nuns attempt to carry foodstuffs and oral
rehydration formulas to outlying villages suffering from diarrhea
and scarce supplies.[130]

---

[130] Article 14 of Protocol II of the Geneva Conventions provides that
"It is ...prohibited to attack, destroy, remove or render useless, for that
purpose, objects indispensable to the survival of the civilian population,
such as foodstuffs, agricultural areas for the production of foodstuffs,
crops, livestock, drinking water installations and supplies and irrigation
works.

On February 18, 1994, a truckload of donated food and medicine accompanied by National Autonomous University of Mexico (UAM) students arrived in Altamirano. After a lengthy search at the military checkpoint, the caravan of students left half of their ten tons of humanitarian aid supplies at the hospital and set out to deliver the remainder to the village of Morelia. When they traversed the center of Altamirano, the caravan and its occupants were surrounded by hundreds of armed and angry demonstrators, reportedly led by Jorge Constantino Kantor, the local PRI strongman. The caravan, the leaders of the demonstration said, would not be permitted to pass because the food and medicine was destined for Zapatistas. For four hours, the crowd heckled and threatened the students, while the leaders of the demonstration demanded to search and inventory the truck's contents. Soldiers, state judicial police, and the mayor did nothing to halt the illegal blockade. Finally, faced with mounting threats to their members from the increasingly belligerent crowd, the caravan's organizers turned over the entire shipment and were allowed to depart, but only after the leaders of the demonstration searched and photographed and recorded the names of the students.

Assault on the Clinic of Morelia

The ejido of Morelia lies approximately seven kilometers east of Altamirano on a rutted dirt road. On the morning of January 7, 1994, a large detachment of army troops descended on this community of 2,000 people allegedly in pursuit of Zapatistas (see Chapter VI). With the soldiers were at least two "informers," fellow villagers who had allegedly fled the ejido over past disputes. While troops routed the villagers out of their houses and herded them to the town's central square, several soldiers set out with an informer to find Humberto Santiz López.[131]

---

[131] PHR representatives interviewed Humberto Santiz López on March 30, 1994.

Santiz was a 32-year-old farmer, whose father, Sebastián Santiz López, owned the village store. The son, Humberto Santiz López, recalls a relative came to his home when the soldiers arrived and told him to go to the basketball court which serves as the village square:

> As I was walking there, a group of about fourteen
> soldiers stopped me. I thought they wanted to ask
> me a question, but one of them ordered, 'Take us
> to your house.' When we got to the house, the
> leader demanded that I give him the key to the
> clinic. I didn't know what to do, I wasn't
> responsible for the clinic...I told them that, but he
> ordered his men to search the house anyway.
> When they couldn't find the key, they marched me
> in the direction of the clinic. As we went up the
> path, they pulled my hair and threw me to the
> ground. When we arrived, I could see there were
> tanks everywhere...They put me up against the
> back wall of the clinic, and said they were going
> to shoot me unless I told them the name of the
> doctor who worked there. 'Her name is
> Alejandra, isn't it?' one of them said. I replied
> that everyone knew that.

Until the rebellion, Morelia was one of the few ejidos that had its own clinic, staffed with a doctor and four nurses. It was rumored that the doctor had since joined the Zapatistas, and the army may have been searching for her as well.

Humberto Santiz López recalls watching the soldiers as they ransacked the clinic:

> Well, [the soldiers] entered the clinic and began
> breaking everything: doors, windows, medicine
> cabinets, equipment. They threw medicines,
> sheets, and even the jackets worn by the doctor
> and nurses, onto the floor. Finally, they came
> across a bundle of papers belonging to one of the

doctors who had worked there. In it was a diploma and some books, which [the soldiers] took with them.

This blatant attack on a health facility and destruction of medical equipment and medicines, presumably because they might have been used or would be used by the Zapatistas, violates Protocol II of the Geneva Conventions of 1949.

Not only were medical facilities targeted by the Mexican army, but the military's own medical personnel, equipment, and even its symbols of neutrality were subverted during counterinsurgency operations in Chiapas. This was the case in Morelia on the afternoon of January 7, when a green army vehicle, bearing a prominent red cross, was used to transport three men who had been tortured by army troops away from the village (see Chapter VI). According to villagers, army troops detained and tortured Severiano Santiz Gómez, Hermelindo Santiz Gómez, and Sebastián Santiz López for several hours in the village church before loading them into what was clearly a military ambulance. The ambulance then left in the direction of Altamirano.

As indicated in Chapter VI, the three men never arrived at military headquarters in Altamirano, but were taken from the military ambulance and murdered (see Appendix A and B). The use of an ambulance for murder represents one of the gravest violations of medical neutrality committed by the Mexican army.

After the army troops departed Morelia, the villagers found themselves almost completely cut off from medical care. While women and children could initially enter Altamirano for food, supplies, and medical care, the alleged rape of three Tzeltal teenage sisters in June at an army checkpoint put even this limited freedom in doubt (see Chapter V). Meanwhile, male villagers who dare to cross through the military roadblocks at the entrance to Altamirano risk arrest and prolonged interrogation. As recently as early August, foreign observers attempting to enter Morelia were told that the so-called "gray zone" which encompassed the village was off-limits to non-Mexicans. Supplies of all types en

route to Morelia have been strictly monitored by soldiers.
Moreover, IMSS vaccination teams have carefully avoided Morelia
on their rounds, claiming security risks to their personnel.
However, IMSS trucks have frequently been spotted driving by the
village on their way to less controversial villages even deeper in
the "gray zone."

Medical Services Denied in Ocosingo

On January 4, 1994, reporters were allowed into the
embattled town of Ocosingo. One of the most horrifying scenes to
emerge that day was footage of a *Televisa* reporter interviewing a
Zapatista rebel as he lay dying in the street. "Let me die," he said
as Mexican soldiers looked on, unconcerned. Army troops had
already removed all of their own dead and wounded from the
street, but guerrilla casualties lay where they had died. And in
this case, a wounded rebel, who later died, was denied medical
care.[132]

American reporters told PHR that they had sought help for
the dying Zapatistas at the IMSS clinic, but were turned away by
military authorities who had already closed the hospital and turned
patients and doctors alike out into the street (see Chapter VI).
The failure of Mexican army to provide emergency medical aid to
enemy soldiers placed hors de combat is a serious violation of the
Geneva Conventions of 1949 and Protocol II, and a breach of
military conduct that the Ministry of Defense (SEDENA) has
never attempted to justify or explain.

The Mexican army also bears responsibility for failing to
provide any medical care for the civilian population in the

---

[132] Article 7 of Protocol II of the Geneva Conventions of 1949
provides: "1. All wounded, sick and shipwrecked, whether or not they
have take part in the armed conflict, shall be respected and protected. 2.
In all circumstances they shall be treated humanely and shall receive, to
the fullest extent practicable and with the least possible delay, the
medical care and attention required by their condition. There shall be no
distinction among them found on any grounds other than medical ones."

aftermath of the battle for Ocosingo. In fact, they were instrumental in denying the entire city necessary medical services exactly when they were most needed. When army soldiers entered the Ocosingo hospital, they ejected doctors, nurses, and patients from the wards directly out onto the streets. On January 12, when the army re-opened Ocosingo to the outside world residents spoke of seeing dazed patients wandering the streets near the clinic clad only in hospital gowns and seeking shelter. In the meantime, all the doctors and nurses at the hospital had fled or had been evacuated by the military.[133]

Late in the afternoon on January 14, the Mexican Red Cross hastily set up a field hospital on the outskirts of Ocosingo. The same day, almost two weeks after the forced closure of the IMSS hospital, a small mobile clinic run by the department of transportation arrived in the central square of Ocosingo.

Stories that emerged from the frightened population of Ocosingo after the city re-opened told an even more terrifying tale. When the army troops stormed Ocosingo on the afternoon of January 2, orders were apparently given to shoot to kill anyone attempting to leave their homes. Investigators heard many stories of civilians who were killed trying to find missing family members or obtain food. One women said her husband was shot by an Army soldier while carrying tortillas home. The woman begged the soldiers to let her take her wounded husband to the hospital, but was told to return to her house with her husband or she, too, would be shot. Her husband later died. When the army refused her permission to transport her husband's body to the cemetery, she buried him in the patio of her home. The Fray Bartolomé de las Casas has documented several cases of patio burials in Ocosingo, as surviving family members have overcome their fear and sought to obtain proper burials for their deceased relatives.

---

[133] On January 12, a delegation from PHR, HRW/Americas, and MAHR travelled to Ocosingo. The delegation was unable to find a single physician in this town of 60,000. Even private doctors had left.

The refusal of the Mexican army to provide the most basic medical needs to the civilian population of Ocosingo in the first days of the conflict needlessly increased the human cost of the conflict.

VIII. CONCLUSIONS AND RECOMMENDATIONS

In recent years, several Mexican officials--civilian and military alike--have professed their commitment to upholding international human right standards and vigorously pursuing those public servants who violate them. Soon after ordering Army troops into Chiapas, President Carlos Salinas de Gortari reiterated his promise to defend human rights. He dispatched the President of the National Commission of Human Rights (CNDH) to Chiapas to oversee all investigations of alleged abuses and to ensure that those responsible would be prosecuted by the competent authorities. Similarly, the Mexican army established offices in several major towns previously occupied by the Ejército Zapatista de Liberación Nacional (EZLN) to receive complaints of army abuses.

At the onset of the rebellion, the EZLN acknowledged that its forces were bound by the Geneva Conventions of 1949, and called on international organizations and the International Committee of the Red Cross (ICRC) to monitor the conflict. EZLN commanders also announced publicly that they had appointed special committees to discipline rebel fighters who violated their internal codes of conduct or the Geneva Conventions.

Such pledges notwithstanding, Physicians for Human Rights (PHR) and Human Rights Watch/Americas (HRW/Americas) have found that both sides in the twelve-day conflict committed serious violations of international humanitarian law as set forth in Article 3 to the Geneva Conventions of 1949.[134] Article 3 provides that civilians and those taking no part in a conflict are to be protected, and that under all circumstances fundamental human rights are to be respected.

---

[134] See Chapter IV.

1. Violations of the Laws of War by the EZLN

During the conflict and its aftermath, EZLN rebels shot and killed noncombatants and took at least six civilian hostages. "Violence to life and person" and the taking of hostages are strictly forbidden under Common Article 3 of the Geneva Conventions of 1949.

- We call on the EZLN to enforce discipline within its ranks in conformity with the Geneva Conventions, which the EZLN leadership has pledged to respect. The EZLN should make public the disciplinary measures taken against its members who have violated international humanitarian law.

- The EZLN officers have the responsibility of instructing their soldiers in the rules of war, especially in Common Article 3 of the Geneva Conventions of 1949 and Protocol II, which describe the rights of the wounded and sick to receive medical care in time of noninternational armed conflict. EZLN officers should also inform those under their command that they will be disciplined for any infringements of international humanitarian law.

2. Violations of Human Rights and Humanitarian Law by the Mexican Army

Mexican army troops were responsible for serious violations of human rights and humanitarian law during the conflict and in its aftermath. These violations include (1) summary executions of wounded or captured combatants, and of civilians in detention; (2) widespread arbitrary arrest, prolonged incommunicado detention, and torture; (3) excessive use of lethal force; and (4) violations of medical neutrality. To date, not one officer has been identified and held responsible for any of these abuses.

During the New Year's Day rebellion and the weeks that followed, the Mexican government never introduced a state of emergency. Nor did it follow the constitutional procedures required for the suspension or limitation of due process and individual guarantees. Therefore, the Mexican army acted unconstitutionally when it assumed apparent *de facto* state of emergency powers. As this report documents, army troops detained, interrogated, and transported civilian suspects without legal warrant; refused civilian access to villages and communities; buried bodies without civilian procedures; and carried out medicolegal investigations, including autopsies, of civilian victims, thereby undermining the authority of responsible civilian officials. These infringements of civilian authority and due process had no basis in Mexican law and violated Mexico's obligations under the International Covenant on Civil and Political Rights.

- The Mexican government should ensure that any acts by either government or EZLN forces which constitute violations of human rights or humanitarian law are fully and independently investigated and that those responsible for such violations are identified and prosecuted in civilian courts. The Mexican government should clarify the amnesty law of January 20, 1994, enacted to ensure that it is not applied to exempt these persons from criminal prosecution or conviction. Moreover, officials with chain-of-command responsibility who ordered or tolerated criminal acts, especially torture, rape, and extrajudicial executions, should be held criminally responsible for those acts.

- The Congress or judiciary should investigate the circumstances in which Mexican armed forces were authorized to disregard and infringe due process and constitutional rights and guarantees during the Chiapas conflict. This investigation should examine the chain-of-command structure to determine at what level such authorization was given. In the future the government should ensure observance of constitutional constraints on the participation of the armed forces in law enforcement activities such as the detention and questioning of suspects, and ensure that due process guarantees are respected at all times.

3. Failure to Conduct Adequate Investigations of Extrajudicial Executions

PHR and HRW/Americas conclude that the two principal federal agencies officially responsible for investigations of extrajudicial executions and other criminal acts committed during the Chiapas rebellion--the federal Attorney General's office (PGR) and the National Commission on Human Rights (CNDH)--have often failed to conduct their work in an independent, thorough, competent, and timely manner, as provided for in the United Nations "Principles on the Effective Prevention and Investigation of Extra-legal, Arbitrary and Summary Executions" (see Appendix C).

In Chapter VI of this report, we examine the investigations by the PGR and CNDH of four separate cases of apparent extrajudicial executions involving as many as twenty-one possible victims. We also present our own forensic observations or findings in three of these cases. We believe that the PGR has often shown a greater interest in protecting the Mexican army's reputation than in conducting independent and thorough investigations. Moreover, the CNDH's integrity has been tarnished by its reluctance to speak out in a forceful and timely manner when it was aware of incompetence, discrepancies, or outright contradictions in the findings and conclusions drawn by the PGR.

PHR forensic specialists found that their counterparts in the CNDH (as opposed to the PGR) were adequately trained, and that they generally conducted medicolegal investigations, including autopsies, in a professional manner[135] PHR forensic specialists were less impressed with the methods and procedures followed by

---

[135] Those standards are set forth in the *Manual on the Effective Prevention and Investigation of Extra-Legal, Arbitrary and Summary Executions*, published by the United Nations Office at Vienna, Centre for Social Development and Humanitarian Affairs in 1991 (U.N. Sales No. E.91.IV.1). The manual is available in English, Spanish, French, Russian, and Arabic.

CNDH and PGR crime scene investigators, who often failed to collect and preserve evidence in a rigorous and thorough manner (see Chapter VI). In general, however, most of these official investigations were not grossly mishandled at the forensic level (though improvements should be made), but rather at a much higher level within the investigating agency's bureaucracy.

PGR and CNDH officials, at the highest levels, have lacked the political will to acknowledge publicly that elements of the military or paramilitary groups may have acted as either perpetrators or accomplices in extrajudicial executions during the Chiapas rebellion. The CNDH, for its part, appears to have chosen not to make public credible eyewitness accounts that clearly implicate military personnel in extrajudicial executions. Nowhere is this more evident than in the investigation of the mass grave in the municipal cemetery in Ocosingo (See chapter VI). HRW/Americas and PHR know that CNDH officials interviewed patients in the Ocosingo hospital who have testified that soldiers abducted or shot civilians on the grounds of the hospital. Even so, the CNDH has made no reference to these testimonies in its public announcements.

With regard to specific cases, we find:

A. Executions in Morelia

Based on the anthropological and preliminary genetic findings of its forensic experts (see Appendices A and B), PHR and HRW/Americas conclude that *prima facie* evidence exists to charge Mexican army personnel in the detention, torture, and murder of Severiano Santiz Gómez, Sebastián Santiz López, and Hermelindo Santiz Gómez who were last seen alive in army custody in the ejido of Morelia on January 7, 1994.

- As a first step, the Mexican government should arrest immediately the army officers who had command responsibility for the

117

counterinsurgency operation in Morelia. Officials suspected of responsibility for these killings should also be suspended from active duty during the investigation.

B. Executions in Ocosingo

HRW/Americas and PHR believe the PGR, in its press bulletins of January 7 and April 7, 1994, has attempted to cover up possible military involvement in the summary executions of five men in the Ocosingo marketplace on January 3 (see Chapter VI). Furthermore, when confronted with contradictions in their findings, including the misidentification of one of the bodies as Pablo Santiz Gómez (see photographs), the PGR failed to reconsider their exoneration of military personnel as possible suspects in these murders.

- Given the gravity of this situation, the Mexican government should appoint immediately an independent, special commission of inquiry to investigate the five killings in the Ocosingo marketplace and the assault on the minibus (see Chapter V & VI), in compliance with the United Nations "Model Protocol for a Legal Investigation of Extra-Legal, Arbitrary and Summary Executions" (see Appendix C).[136] The special commission should also investigate the manner in which the PGR generally conducted

---

[136] *Ibid.*, pp. 15-23.

death investigations pertaining
to the Chiapas rebellion and its
aftermath.

The Mexican government should
order all civilian and military
agencies to turn over their
documentation and evidence
pertaining to these cases to the
special commission of inquiry.
The commission's terms of reference
should include the authority to
compel testimony under legal
sanction and to order the
production of documents including
government and medical records.

PHR and HRW/Americas recognize that the CNDH is an
ombudsmen's office, charged not to prosecute but to ensure that
investigations by other investigatory agencies are conducted in a
prompt, thorough, and impartial manner. Even so, we are
concerned that since February 1994 the CNDH has failed to make
any recommendations to the PGR and the military prosecutor's
office regarding the extrajudicial executions documented in this
report. This silence is especially troubling as we know, for
instance, that the CNDH is well aware of the contradictions
apparent in the PGR's findings in the five killings in the Ocosingo
marketplace and the assault on the minibus.

- We call on the CNDH to release
  its findings and recommendations
  in a timely manner, even if they
  contradict conclusions drawn by
  other agencies, governmental or
  otherwise.

EXAMINATION OF HUMAN SKELETAL REMAINS FOUND NEAR MORELIA, CHIAPAS ON FEBRUARY 10, 1994

Clyde Collins Snow, Ph.D.
and
Thomas Crane, M.D.

CASE SUMMARY

These human remains, which were recovered from a ravine near Morelia, Chiapas, are those of three indigenous males who died from multiple blunt force trauma one to three months prior to the discovery of the remains on February 10, 1994. The remains are generally consistent with Hermelindo Santiz Gómez, Severiano Santiz Gómez, and Sebastián Santiz López. All three men were last seen alive in the custody of the Mexican army in the ejido of Morelia on January 7, 1994.

Examination Procedures

The human remains had been stored in a single wooden coffin which was brought to the examination room and opened in the presence of the authors. The bones were removed from the coffin and laid out on a separate table. Preliminary inspection revealed four nonhuman bones; the rest were obviously human. Cranial bones were then separated from the assemblage and placed on a separate examination table. Another table was reserved for ribs and vertebra.

The cranial fragments were found to include portions of three skulls (designated here as **Mor1, Mor2, Mor3**). The numerous detached cranial fragments were studied to assign them to their parent skulls. Cranial reconstruction was accomplished with the aid of an electric glue gun. After the reconstructions were complete, all three skulls displayed major defects representing fragments which had not been recovered. The postcranial remains were sorted anatomically.

Due to extreme fragmentation, most standard osteometric measurements could not be taken. Items of interest were photographed in 35mm color. The three skulls were X-rayed to determine the presence of possible bullet fragments. Extraction and preservation of teeth for DNA analysis followed the collection protocol established by the genetic laboratories of Dr. Mary-Claire King at the School of Public Health, University of California, Berkeley.

Antemortem information was obtained in interviews with the family members of the missing men. In soliciting this information, a protocol developed by the Argentine Forensic Anthropology Team and Physician for Human Rights was followed. A Tzeltal-speaking interpreter was present to help with informants who were not fluent in Spanish.

OBSERVATIONS

Inventory

The assemblage contained 118 bones which could be anatomically identified and, in the case of bilateral elements, assigned to one side or another (**Table 1**). In addition, there were twenty-one fragments too small to classify and a fully ossified thyroid cartilage. It was evident that the assemblage represented the commingled remains of *at least* three skeletons since seven anatomical subsets (cranium, mandible, left clavicle, right humerus, left innominate, left femur, right femur) contained three bones.

The 118 identified bones constitute only about twenty-two percent of 540 bones[137] in three adult human skeletons. This low recovery rate is a reflection of the extensive postmortem fragmentation and wide dispersal of the remains by the animal scavengers. The difficult terrain and dense vegetation of the discovery area also hampered recovery.

Because many bones were missing entirely and nearly all of those recovered had been partially destroyed by scavengers, only a few could be assigned to individual skeletons on the basis of articulation and morphological consistency. It is also impossible to associate any of the postcranial bones with a particular skull.

Condition

The cortical surfaces of most of the bones were still largely covered with tattered relics of dried periosteal membrane. Disarticulation was complete except for some short vertebral segments and a left innominate and femur. Attached to the latter was a large piece of partially mummified skin and muscle tissue. The strong, slightly sour odor of advanced decomposition clung to the remains. Cortical surfaces were greasy to the touch, indicating that the bones still retained a considerable amount of fat. The bones varied from dark-grey or brown to near-white in color. There were no signs of cortical erosion or weathering usually associated with prolonged exposure.

Postmortem damage by scavengers was extensive. Except for the three mandibula, sixteen ribs, and the left patella. All of the bones had been partially destroyed. In all of the twenty-six long bones recovered, at least one--and usually both--extremities had been chewed away. This pattern of chewing away the

---

[137] The human skeleton is composed of approximately 200 bones. But for the purpose of recovery analysis in forensic cases, the 21 cranial bones are counted as a single unit reducing the count to 180. See CC. Snow and E.D. Folk, "The statistical assessment of commingled skeletal remains," *American Journal of Physical Anthropology* 1970; 32:423-427.

thinner-walled cancellous bones and sparing the thicker shafts is typical of canid scavengers.

Some of the fragmented bones bore tooth marks which, judging from their size and spacing, were produced by small to medium sized canids. Most indigenous households in this area include several, usually rather small, mixed-breed dogs which are allowed to roam freely in order to supplement a meager diet of table scraps with whatever they can scavenge in the wild. On our visit to the scene, we found the fully-articulated and undisturbed skeleton of a small dog. Its bones displayed no signs of trauma or post-mortem scavenger damage, so it presumably died of natural causes. Since canine scavengers do not ordinarily feed on their own dead, it would appear that local semi-feral "household" dogs or, perhaps, coyotes (*Canis latrans*) were responsible for most of the damage. Carrion-feeding birds such as the Black Vulture (*Coragyps atratus*), Turkey Buzzard (*Cathartes aura*) and American Raven (*Corvus corax*) are also very common in this area. Several shed vulture feathers signified the presence of these birds at the scene. Although these avian scavengers are unable to do much damage to the larger bones, they can strip a human body of its most of its soft parts within a few days. Large quantities of insect pupal cases were present in the loose debris accompanying the remains.

OSTEOLOGY

Skull Mor1

Sex: Morphological features are strongly **masculine**. The mastoid process is robust and nuchal ridges moderate with a medium external occciptal protuberance. Other male characteristics include the strong temporal ridges, blunt inferior orbital margins, large teeth, and strongly squared anterior mandibular border.

Race: Racial features are **mongoloid**. These include the relatively broad and high cranial vault, massive and anteriorly flaring malars, broad nasal aperture, fasciculate inferior nasal margins, slight alveolar prognathism, broad maxillary dental arch, shallow palate, shovel-shaped incisors, and the relatively broad, low mandibular rami.

Age: The frontal and occipital sutures display early closure. The sagittal is largely patent. Alveolar regression and dental attrition are advanced, especially in the molars where wear has resulted in the nearly complete loss of cuspal features. These findings suggest an age at death somewhere in the range of **30 to 45 years.**

Dentition (Table 2): With the exception of the right maxillary third molar, the dentition was complete at the time of death. In the mandible, the left central incisor, both right incisors and the right second molar are missing postmortem. Caries is confined to occlusal foveal pits in the maxillary left third and right second molars. Periodontal disease is advanced. No dental restorations are present. The teeth are heavily tobacco-stained.

Skull Mor2

Sex: Cranial morphology is **masculine.** This diagnosis is based on the robust supraorbital brow ridges, marked temporal crests, large mastoid processes, well-developed nuchal ridges with a prominent external occipital protuberance, blunt superior orbital margins, deeply depressed nasal root, large teeth, deep anterior mandible, and a prominent and salient chin.

Race: Racial features are predominately **mongoloid.** These include the broad and high cranial vault, simple cranial suture pattern, broad and low nasal root, strong and angular zygomatic bone (only the right is present), and wide, low mandibular rami.

Age: Cranial vault sutures show early ectocranial but complete endocranial closure. Antemortem dental loss, alveolar regression and dental wear are advanced. Based on these findings, the age at death is estimated to have been between **45 and 65 years.**

Dentition (Table 2): The maxillary dentition is represented only by a small portion of the left posterior alveolus. This fragment contains the roots of the second molar; the third molar was lost postmortem. In the mandible, both first molars and the right second premolar are missing antemortem. All the remaining teeth are missing premortem, except four in the right quadrant: canine, first premolar, second and third molars. The four remaining teeth are moderately worn and heavily tobacco-stained. There is a small carious lesion on the proximo-occlusal margin of the right second molar. Periodontal disease is advanced. The left central incisor was disto-buccally rotated and the lateral displaced posteriorly--features that might be recalled by the decedent's relatives or would be displayed in a smiling photograph.

Skull Mor3

Sex: Morphological features are strongly **masculine**, with a strong supraorbital brow ridge, large mastoid, well-developed nuchal ridges, large external occipital protuberance, deeply depressed nasal root, large teeth and robust mandible.

Race: Cranial racial traits are typically **mongoloid**. These include the rather broad, high, cranial vault and simple vault suture pattern. The molars are prominent and angular. The orbits are low and angular, the nasal bridge is wide and low, the nasal aperture is broad with a guttered inferior nasal margin. The mandibular rami are low and broad.

Age: Cranial suture closure is moderately advanced. Antemortem tooth loss is extensive and the remaining teeth are well worn. Based on these findings, the age at death is placed between **45 and 70 years.**

Dentition (Table 2): The maxilla is edentulous. The "knife-edge" alveolar borders suggest these teeth were lost at least several years prior to death. A full upper denture found with the remains fits the maxilla (**Fig. 1**).

In the left mandibular quadrant, the first and second molars are missing antemortem, the left second premolar displays massive caries; the remaining teeth are present. In the right quadrant, the central incisor has been lost postmortem, the lateral incisor and canine are present.

The most striking feature of this dentition is the five-unit fixed bridge of rather unusual design in the right mandibular quadrant (**Fig. 2**). It is abutted on the second premolar and third molar. From the premolar abutment, a cantilevered proximal extension replaces the 1st premolar. The abutted teeth are jacketed with full white-metal crowns; the pontic and cantilever replacements are three-quarter white-metal with porcelain-type lingual facings.

The quality and workmanship in both the bridge and the upper prothesis are very poor. However, dental restorations of any kind are relatively rare among local indigenes and suggests that this individual was, by Morelian standards, of somewhat higher than average socioeconomic status.

Postcranial Bones

Although most of the postcranial elements could not be assigned to individual skeletons, the collection as a whole displayed features consistent with the age, sex and racial features observed in the skulls. For example, the vertebrae displayed moderate to advanced osteophytosis typical in individuals over 40 years of age. In the few bones where articular surfaces were preserved, osteoarthritic changes also suggest individuals middle-aged or older.

Observable morphological features were **masculine**. Thus, all of the innominate fragments displayed relatively narrow sciatic notches and, in one with the ischium and pubis still intact, the pubic angle was acute, the ischiopubic border everted and the

126

symphysis subquandrangular. Other postcranial bones displayed heavy musculature attachment markings. In the femora, the shafts showed the anterior bowing and platymeria[138] typical of indigenes of this region.

None of the long bones were sufficiently intact to permit measurements necessary to calculate antemortem stature. However from the general size of the bones it was evident that all three individuals were relatively short and well within the statural range of 156.3 /plus or minus 5.1 cm. of Tzeltal males.[139]

Antemortem fractures were present on three lower right ribs. Morphological consistencies indicated that these ribs (probably the ninth, tenth and eleventh) were from the same skeleton. All three fractures were located in the proximal third of the shafts, suggesting that they resulted from a single traumatic episode. None of the remaining postcranial bones bore signs of antemortem trauma or disease.

PERIMORTEM TRAUMA

Turkey vultures and coyotes often make life difficult for forensic anthropologists by adding to the difficulty of detecting and interpreting evidence of perimortem violence. First, by widely scattering the bony remains, they virtually insure that some will elude discovery in even the most diligent scene search. For example, when large portions of the skull are missing, it leaves

---

[138] Transverse flattening of the upper third of the diaphysis.

[139] Based on the combined anthropometric data on 197 Tzeltal males from the studies of Starr and of Leche *et al.* (see Starr, F. Notes upon the ethnography of southern Mexico, Part 2. *Proceedings of the Davenport Academy of Natural Sciences* 9: 107.1902. and Leche, H.N., Gould, N. and D. Tharp. Dermatoglyphics and functional lateral dominance in Mexican Indians. V. Zinancantecs, Huixtecs, Amatenangos, and Finca Tzeltals. *Tulane University, Middle American Research Institute,* Pub. 15, pp. 21-84, 1944.). The average height of 25 females measured by Starr was 143.8 centimeters.

the nagging question of whether one of the unrecovered fragments might have held a clue to the cause of death--a bullet hole or perhaps an impression fracture left by a bludgeoning weapon such as hammer or pistol butt. Also, in the bones that are found, damage superimposed by scavengers may obscure patterns of trauma inflicted at the time of death.

Fortunately, familiarity with the capabilities and proclivities of carrion-feeding scavengers helps clarify the picture of perimortem trauma. For example, the jaws of even the largest canids are not capable of producing much damage to the stouter parts of the skeleton of a healthy human adult.[140] In the long bones of the arm and leg, for example, they cannot break the thick diaphysial shafts. Instead, they are forced to concentrate their chewing, gnawing and nibbling on the thin-walled ends of the bones where they usually leave tell-tale clues in the form of tooth marks. Smaller and more fragile postcranial elements, such as the ribs, scapulae and the small bones of the hands and feet are also vulnerable and may be almost totally destroyed.

In the skull, scavengers can wreak heavy damage to the thin and delicate bones of the upper and middle parts of the facial skeleton but can do little harm to the more robustly structured zygomatic bones and mandible. The thick, tightly interlocked bones of the cranial vault initially gives good protection to the brain but later, after the nuchal musculature has disappeared and ligamentous decomposition permits separation of the skull from the vertebral column, the thinner bones of the exposed cranial base may be provide access to the cranial cavity and its contents. The foramen magnum is often the first focus of attacks on the cranial base and the bone surrounding it will be broken away in order to enlarge the portal of access to the endocranium.

---

[140] A notable exception being the Spotted Hyaena (*Crocuta crocuta*) of sub-Saharan Africa whose powerful jaws and digestive juices enable them to make short work of very large bones.

Skull Mor1 (Fig. 3a-e)

This skull[141] displays massive fractures of the cranial vault, base and upper face. About forty percent of the surface area of the neurocranium is missing, leaving three gaping defects in the frontal, right parietal and in a confluent area of the lower left cranial vault and cranial base.

The remaining cranial vault shows a complex network of branching fractures. One set extends from the rear margin of the frontal defect into the parietals where they join fracture lines in that area. Another passes transversely across the parieto-occipital region. In the facial skeleton, a linear fracture of the maxilla extends downward from the right side of the inferior margin of the nasal aperture to the alveolar border between the right central and lateral incisors; it then passes posteriorly through the palate. The mandible is intact.

The fracture margins are abrupt and clean, signifying that they occurred perimortem and were not caused by scavenger depredation. Such massively comminuted fractures are most often the result of high-velocity gunshot wounds or massive blunt force trauma. The first diagnosis appears unlikely since none of the fracture margins display the beveling produced by bullets and X-rays were negative for embedded metal; however, it cannot be ruled out entirely because such features might have been present in the missing fragments. It is more likely that the injuries resulted from blunt force inflicted by one or more blows to the head.

Skull Mor2 (Fig. 4a-d)

Scavengers have destroyed nearly the entire facial skeleton and penetrated the anterior part of the cranial base. The mandible bears no signs of scavenger damage.

---

[141] A note on terminology: As used here, the *skull* refers to the cranium and mandible. The *cranium* is the cranial vault and facial skeleton. The *neurocranium* is the brain case (*neurocranium*).

Neurocranial trauma is limited to the right temporal bone which displays multiple fractures of the squamous portion and a complete fracture of the zygomatic arch. The facial skeleton is missing except for the right zygomatic, the nasal-maxillary root, and a small fragment of the posterior left alveolus. The zygomatic displays a complete linear fracture passing downward and laterally from the mid-point of the inferior orbital margin to the zygomaxillary tubercle. The mandible is divided by three fractures. One fracture passes vertically through the middle of the right mandibular corpus and a second through the chin just right of the midline. The third runs downward and forward from the left coronal margin of the right ramus to the midpoint of the inferior margin of the corpus.

The linear fractures of the mandible denote forces clearly beyond the capabilities of local scavengers and can be confidently diagnosed as the result of perimortem blunt force trauma. The fractures of the right zygomatic and temporal bones are also perimortem. None of these fractures displayed characteristics typical of gunshot wounds and radiological examination showed no embedded metal fragments. Therefore, the observed perimortem injuries are most likely the result of blunt force trauma. The multiple mandibular fractures indicate the injuries were caused by at least two blows to the facial region delivered from different directions.

Skull Mor3 (Fig. 5a-f)

This skull is extensively fragmented and about thirty percent of the surface area of the neurocranium is missing. The area of missing bone is confluent and takes in the left temporal parietal area. Most of the mid-part of the cranial base and extends into lower right side to include most of the temporal bone and smaller parts of the parietal and occipital. The facial skeleton is complete except for some small defects of the zygomatic bones. The mandibular left ramus is missing.

The remaining neurocranial bones show a complex system of fractures. In the anterior vault, there is a 4 x 11 mm.

130

obliquely-oriented, rectangular defect in the lower third of the frontal bone, just left of the midline (**Fig. 6**). Linear fractures arise from both ends of this defect. They pass transversely across the frontal and then send branches posteriorly. The regular shape and sharp margins of the rectangular frontal defect indicate that it was punched out by an object of similar size and shape.

The fractures of the facial skeleton resulted in complete cranio-maxillary disunion (Le Fort's fracture). There is also a fracture of the anterior maxilla passing downward from the medial angle of the nasal aperture to the alveolar border. The mandible displays two complete fractures. One separates the left ramus (which is missing) from the mandibular body. The other originates on the alveolar border between the right lateral incisor and the canine and passes downward to a point on the inferior border just right of the mental protuberance.

All of the fractures observed in this skull were the result of massive blunt force trauma. Radiological examination revealed no embedded metal fragments. The extent and complexity of the fracture pattern suggest multiple blows delivered with great force. The weapon used to inflict the frontal fracture bore a small structure close to the exact size and shape of the rectangular defect.

Postcranial bones

Several bones show diaphysial fractures produced by forces clearly beyond those which animal scavengers are able to exert. One of these was a right humerus with a torsion fracture of the upper third. A right radius and ulna displayed transverse distal fractures at the same level of their diaphysial shafts; morphological features indicated that both of these bones belonged to the same individual and that both bones were broken with a single blow. A comminuted midshaft fracture is present on a left femur. It is also possible that some of the rib fractures were perimortem but scavenger damage makes this determination difficult.

131

TIME OF DEATH

An estimate of the time of death must be based on the state of decomposition which, in turn, is a result of the interaction of many environmental factors. Among the latter are temperature, rainfall, surface vegetation, and the presence and relative abundance of scavengers. The condition of the body itself also affects the rate of decomposition; for example, clothing usually retards decomposition while the presence of open wounds accelerates it by providing portals of access to saprophytic bacteria and insects.

Morelia is in an area of seasonally dry uplands. Winter is the dry season with daytime temperatures ranging between twenty-five and thirty-five degrees Celsius (C°) and nighttime lows of about fifteen to twenty degrees C°. In such a mild climate, sarcophagous insects are active year-round. As noted previously, avian and mammalian carrion-feeders are abundant in this area. The massive perimortem cranial fractures would allow early access to scavengers. Under these conditions, the skeletonization would be rapid. Considering these factors, the time of death is estimated at about one to three months prior to the discovery of the remains.

CAUSE OF DEATH

All three skulls display evidence of severe perimortem blunt force trauma. Complete fractures of the diaphyseal shafts observed in several of the long bones were also inflicted perimortem. Without prompt medical intervention, the head injuries were sufficiently severe to have caused death within a few minutes to a few hours after they were inflicted.

IDENTIFICATION

The skeletal remains were found approximately five kilometers from Morelia. The site is located close to the road connecting Morelia and Altamirano. When the men were taken from Morelia the military vehicle transporting them was seen leaving on that road. From the condition of the remains, the time of death is estimated at one to three months prior to their discovery. No other persons are known to have gone missing from the local area during that time period. Some of the clothing found at the scene matched those worn by the men at the time of their disappearance. Therefore, the three men can be considered *presumed decedents,* and thus they all can be treated as the *restricted* type.[142]

Antemortem Descriptions

No dental or medical records were available on the three men and all of the antemortem descriptions were elicited from family members. As might be expected, this information was somewhat vague and imprecise.

The youngest, **Hermelindo Santiz Gómez,** was an agricultural worker who was 42 years old at the time of his disappearance on January 7. While he was being carried to the military vehicle, bystanders noticed that he had a large bleeding scalp wound in the forehead. He was about 165 cm. tall and weighed about fifty kilograms. So far as relatives were aware, he had never had any broken bones and the only significant injury he had ever sustained was a machete wound of the left hand. He had no dental work and his teeth were in good condition except for

---

[142] From the standpoint of establishing identification, cases can be treated as *restricted, semi-restricted,* or *unrestricted. Restricted* cases are those in which the number of presumed decedents matches the number of bodies (or skeletons) recovered. In *semi-restricted* cases, the number of presumed decedents does not match the number of bodies. *Unrestricted* cases are those in which there are no presumed decedents at the time of examination. Using the Morelia case as an example, it is classified as *restricted* since there are three men known to be missing and three skeletons are represented in the recovered assemblage of skeletal remains. Had four men been reported missing but only three skeletons recovered, it would be classified as *semi-restricted.* If no one at all had been reported missing, it would be classified as *unrestricted.* The distinctions are important since they dictate the approach and limitations of the identification process.

three missing lower incisors. He was a smoker, and his health was good at the time of his disappearance.

The second man was **Severiano Santiz Gómez,** a 59-year-old brick layer at the time of his disappearance. He was about 160 cm. tall and weighed approximately fifty-five kilograms. About five years previously he had suffered an injury to the right thorax in a fall from a scaffold; although it was very painful, he did not seek medical treatment. Most of his teeth were present and he had recently been complaining of dental pain in the left lower jaw. He had no dental work. He was a tobacco smoker. He was in good health at the time of his disappearance.

Sebastián Santiz López was 65 years old at the time of his disappearance. When he was taken to the military vehicle, he was supported by two soldiers. He was 160 cm tall and weighed sixty-three kilograms. He had never suffered any significant skeletal injuries. About twelve years previously, his upper teeth were replaced by a full denture and a metal fixed bridge placed in the lower right jaw. This work was done by a dentist, Dr. Artemio Ballinas, who resides in Altamirano.

Identification

On the basis of the above information, the skeletal remains fit the description of the three men in terms of age, sex, and race. Although antemortem stature could not be estimated precisely from long bone lengths, our assessment of the general body sizes of the individuals represented in the postcranial bones is consistent with the reported small antemortem stature of the three missing men.

Skull Mor1 best fits the available data on **Hermelindo Sántiz Gomez** in terms of age and dental description. It is also interesting to note that witnesses say that he was bleeding from a substantial wound of the forehead when last seen alive; and **Skull Mor1** displayed a fracture in this area. The age estimate for **Mor1** also matches Hermelindo's age more closely than the other two skulls.

A troublesome inconsistency, however, is the antemortem information that Hermelindo had lost three mandibular incisors. In the skull, three mandibular incisors are indeed missing but their open sockets indicate that they were lost postmortem. It is possible, of course, that the crowns of these teeth had been destroyed in life by either trauma or caries, leaving only their roots which fell out after death. Arguing against this interpretation is that the unopposed upper incisors have not dropped beyond the general occlusal plane. It is also possible that the antemortem information was inaccurate or badly translated.

For this reason, the identification of this skull as that of Hermelindo must be considered provisional until confirmed by DNA testing.

The age estimate of **Skull Mor2** is most consistent with **Severiano Santiz Gómez**. It is possible that the three ribs bearing antemortem fractures correlate with Severiano's injury to the right thorax sustained in his accidental fall. However, identification of this individual must also be deemed provisional until confirmed with DNA analysis.

Skull Mor3, with its full upper denture and fixed lower bridge, can be identified as that of **Sebastián Santiz López** with reasonable scientific certainty.

SUMMARY AND CONCLUSIONS

This assemblage contains the commingled remains of three middle-aged indigenous males who died from multiple blunt force trauma one to three months prior to the discovery of the remains on February 10, 1994. The remains are generally consistent with three men who disappeared from Morelia on January 7, 1994.

Skulls Mor1 and **Mor2** are *provisionally* identified as **Hermelindo Santiz Gómez** and **Severiano Santiz Gómez**, respectively. On the basis of dental evidence, **Skull Mor3** is identified as that of **Sebastián Santiz López**.

TABLE 1
INVENTORY AND ANATOMICAL DISTRIBUTION OF BONES
OF MORELIA ASSEMBLAGE

REGION	BONE	Lft.	Rgt.	No.
SKULL	Cranium	-	-	3
	Mandible	-	-	3
	Hyoid	-	-	0
SPINE	Cervical	-	-	4
	Thoracic	-	-	10
	Lumbar	-	-	8
	Sacrum	-	-	1
	Coccyx	-	-	0
THORAX	Sternum	-	-	0
	Ribs	30	23	53
ARM	Clavicle	3	2	5
	Scapula	2	2	4
	Humerus	1	3	4
	Radius	1	1	2
	Ulna	1	1	2
	Hand	0	0	0
LEG	Innominate	3	2	5
	Femur	3	3	6
	Patella	1	0	1
	Tibia	2	2	4
	Fibula	1	2	3
	Foot	0	0	0
ANATOMICALLY CLASSIFIED				118
Unidentified fragments				21
TOTAL				139

136

Table 2
DENTAL CHARTS OF MORELIA SKULLS

Maxilla	#	Toot	Mor1	Mor2	Mor3		Abbreviations
right	1	M3	xam	xpm	rpl		Abbreviations
	2	M2	p	rt	rpl		p: present
	3	M1	p	nr	rpl		xam: lost antemortem
	4	PM2	p	nr	rpl		xpm: lost postmortem
	5	PM1	p	nr	rpl		rpl: replaced
	6	C	p	nr	rpl		crn: crown
	7	I2	p	nr	rpl		car: caries
	8	I1	p	nr	rpl		rt: roots only
left	9	I1	p	nr	rpl		nr: not recovered
	10	I2	p	nr	rpl		
	11	C	p	nr	rpl		
	12	PM1	p	nr	rpl		
	13	PM2	p	nr	rpl		
	14	M1	p	nr	rpl		
	15	M2	p	nr	rpl		
	16	M3	p	nr	rpl		
Mandible							
left	17	M3	p	xpm	p		
	18	M2	p	xpm	xam		
	19	M1	p	xam	xam		
	20	PM2	p	xpm	+5car		
	21	PM1	p	xpm	p		
	22	C	p	xpm	p		
	23	I2	p	xpm	p		
	24	I1	xpm	xpm	p		
right	25	I1	xpm	xpm	xpm		
	26	I2	xpm	xpm	p		
	27	C	p	p	p		
	28	PM1	p	p	rpl		
	29	PM2	p	xpm	crn		
	30	M1	p	xam	rpl		
	31	M2	xpm	p	rpl		
	32	M3	p	p	crn		

137

Fig.1: Occlusal view of upper denture and mandible of skull Mor3

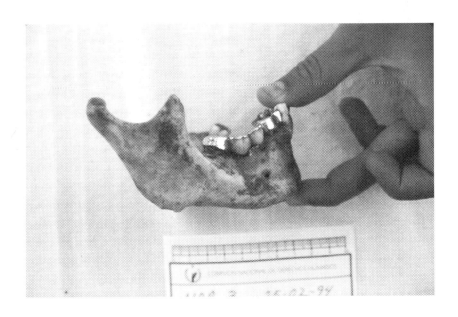

Fig. 2: Right lateral view of mandible of skull Mor3

Fig. 3a-e: Fracture pattern diagram of skull Mor1

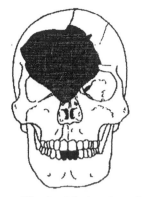

Fig. 3a. Mor1 *n. frontalis*

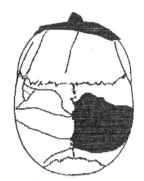

Fig. 3b. Mor1, *n. verticalis*

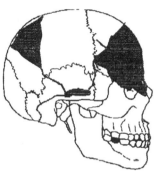

Fig. 3c. Mor1, *n. lateralis dex.*

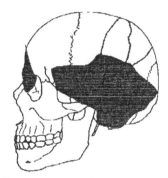

Fig. 3d. Mor1, *n. lateralis sin.*

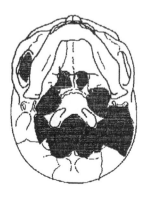

Fig. 3e Mor1, *n. basalaris*

139

Fig. 4a-d: Fracture pattern diagram of skull Mor2

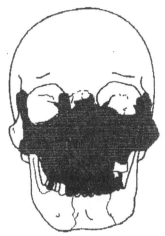

Fig. 4a Mor2, *n. frontalis*

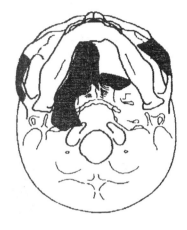

Fig. 4b. Mor2, *n. basalaris*

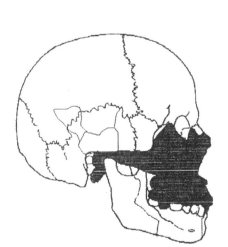

Fig. 4c. Mor2, *n. lateralis dex.*

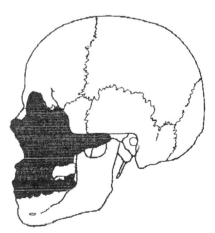

Fig. 4d. Mor2, *n. lateralis sin.*

140

Fig. 5a-f Fracture pattern diagram of skull Mor3

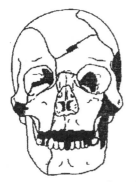

Fig. 5a. Mor3, *n. frontalis*

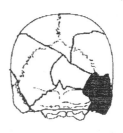

Fig. 5b. Mor3, *n. occiptalis*

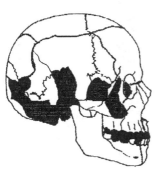

Fig. 5c. Mor3, *n. lateralis dex.*

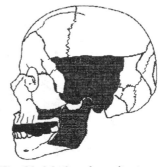

Fig. 5d. Mor3, *n. lateralis sin.*

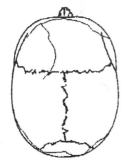

Fig. 5e. Mor3, *n. verticalis*

Fig. 5f. Mor3, *n. basilaris*

Fig. 6: Anterior view of cranium Mor3 showing impression defect on
frontal bone

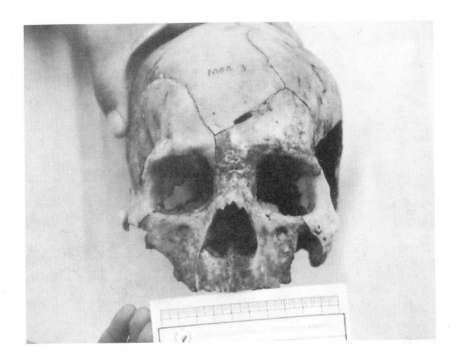

APPENDIX B

UNIVERSITY OF CALIFORNIA, BERKELEY

BERKELEY · DAVIS · IRVINE · LOS ANGELES · RIVERSIDE · SAN DIEGO · SANFRANCISCO   SANTA BARBARA · SANTA CRUZ

349 Mulford Hall
Mary-Claire King, PhD   510-642-4100 phone
American Cancer Society Professor of Genetics and Epidemiology   510-642-0687 fax
Department of Molecular & Cell Biology and School of Public Health   king@mendel.berkeley.edu

November 15, 1994

Eric Stover, Executive Director
Physicians for Human Rights
100 Boylston Street, Suite 702
Boston MA 02116

Dear Mr Stover,

It has been an honor to work with PHR and especially with Tom Crane and Clyde Snow on the identification of remains from Chiapas. We enclose the analysis of tooth #1 and tooth #2. As you know, our approach is to obtain DNA from the tooth and to sequence regions 1 and 2 of the origin of replication of mitochondrial DNA (reference: Ginther C, Issel-Tarver L, King M-C. 1992. Identifying individuals by sequencing mtDNA from teeth. Nature Genetics 2:135-138). The enclosed table indicates all variant sites among the 625 nucleotides of the critical sequence.

The mtDNA sequence of tooth #1 matches the comparable sequences of Jesus Santis Gomez (blood #2) and Virginia Santis Gomez (blood #3), the brother and sister of Severiano Santis Gomez. The mtDNA sequence of tooth #2 matches the comparable sequences of Domingo Santis Gomez (blood #4) and Virginia Santis Gomez (blood #5). The analysis of tooth #3 is still in progress.

It is not yet possible to attach an exact probability of a coincidental match for either tooth #1 or tooth #2, because our analysis of mtDNA sequences from multiple members of the Chiapas population is not yet complete. However, we can confirm

(1) that the mtDNA sequence of tooth #1 is consistent with these remains being Severiano Santis Gomez, and

(2) that the mtDNA sequence of tooth #2 is consistent with these remains being Hermelindo Santis Gomez.

We will of course keep you informed of additional results as our work progresses. We send our best wishes to the families of these victims, and our conviction that their courage in pursuing the murderers of their relatives will make the next would-be murderers think twice and perhaps save someone's life.

Sincerely,

Mary-Claire King

Mary-Claire King

mtDNA sequences from teeth of murder victims and possible relatives from Chiapas

Sample	Name	16093	16129	16223	16240	16290	16294	16295	16298	16319	16325	16327	16362	64	73	146	153	214	235	249	253	263	290-291
consensus		T	G	C	A	C	C	C	T	G	T	C	T	T	A	T	A	A	A	A	C	A	AA
Tooth 1	Severiano Santis Gomez ?	C	A	T	A	C	C	C	C	G	C	T	T	C	G	T	A	G	A	0	C	G	00
Blood 2	Jesus Santis Gomez	C	A	T	A	C	C	C	C	G	C	T	T	C	?	T	A	G	A	0	?	G	00
Blood 3	Virginia Santis Gomez	C	A	T	A	C	C	C	C	G	C	T	T	C	?	T	A	G	A	0	?	G	00
Tooth 2	Hermelindo Santis Gomez ?	T	G	T	G	T	T	T	T	A	T	C	C	T	G	C	G	A	G	A	C	G	AA
Blood 4	Domingo Santis Gomez	T	G	T	G	T	T	T	T	A	T	C	C	T	?	C	G	A	G	A	C	G	AA
Blood 5	Virginia Santis Gomez	T	G	T	G	T	T	T	T	A	T	C	C	T	?	C	G	A	G	A	C	G	AA

0 indicates deletion; ? indicates sequence not clear at this nucleotide

144

APPENDIX C

III. MODEL PROTOCOL FOR A LEGAL INVESTIGATION OF EXTRA-LEGAL,
ARBITRARY AND SUMMARY EXECUTIONS ("MINNESOTA PROTOCOL")

A. Introduction

Suspected extra-legal, arbitrary and summary executions can be investigated under established national or local laws and can lead to criminal proceedings. In some cases, however, investigative procedures may be inadequate because of the lack of resources and expertise or because the agency assigned to conduct the investigation may be partial. Hence, such criminal proceedings are less likely to be brought to a successful outcome.

The following comments may enable those conducting investigations and other parties, as appropriate, to obtain some in-depth guidance for conducting investigations. Such guidance in a general way, has been set out in the Principles on the Effective Prevention and Investigation of Extra-Legal, Arbitrary and Summary Executions (see annex I, below, paragraphs 9-17). The guidelines set forth in this proposed model protocol for a legal investigation of extra-legal, arbitrary and summary executions are not binding. Instead, the model protocol is meant to be illustrative of methods for carrying out the standards enumerated in the Principles.

By definition, this model protocol cannot be exhaustive as the variety of legal and political arrangements escapes its application. Also, investigative techniques vary from country to country and these cannot be standardized in the form of internationally adopted principles. Consequently, additional comments may be relevant for the practical implementation of the Principles.

Sections B and C of this model protocol contain guidelines for the investigation of all violent, sudden, unexpected or suspicious deaths, including suspected extra-legal, arbitrary and summary executions. These guidelines apply to investigations conducted by law enforcement personnel and by members of an independent commission of inquiry.

Section D provides guidelines for establishing a special independent commission of inquiry. These guidelines are based on the experiences of several countries that have established independent commissions to investigate alleged arbitrary executions.

Several considerations should be taken into account when a Government decides to establish an independent commission of inquiry. First, persons subject to an inquiry should be guaranteed the minimum procedural safeguards protected by international law* at all stages of the investigation. Secondly, investigators should have the support of adequate technical and administrative personnel, as well as access to objective, impartial legal advice to ensure that the investigation will produce admissible evidence for later criminal proceedings. Thirdly, investigators should receive the full scope of the Government's resources and powers. Finally, investigators should have the power to seek help from the international community of experts in law, medicine and forensic sciences.

_____

*In particular, all persons must be guaranteed the due process rights set forth in article 14 of the International Covenant on Civil and Political Rights.

The fundamental principles of any viable investigation into the causes of death are competence, thoroughness, promptness and impartiality of the investigation, which flow from paragraphs 9 and 11 of the Principles. These elements can be adapted to any legal system and should guide all investigations of alleged extra-legal, arbitrary and summary executions.

B. Purposes of an inquiry

As set out in paragraph 9 of the Principles, the broad purpose of an inquiry is to discover the truth about the events leading to the suspicious death of a victim. To fulfil this purpose, those conducting the inquiry shall, at a minimum, seek:

(a) To identify the victim;

(b) To recover and preserve evidentiary material related to the death to aid in any potential prosecution of those responsible;

(c) To identify possible witnesses and obtain statements from them concerning the death;

(d) To determine the cause, manner, location and time of death, as well as any pattern or practice that may have brought about the death;

(e) To distinguish between natural death, accidental death, suicide and homicide;

(f) To identify and apprehend the person(s) involved in the death;

(g) To bring the suspected perpetrator(s) before a competent court established by law.

C. Procedures of an inquiry

One of the most important aspects of a thorough and impartial investigation of an extra-legal, arbitrary and summary execution is the collection and analysis of evidence. It is essential to recover and preserve physical evidence, and to interview potential witnesses so that the circumstances surrounding a suspicious death can be clarified.

1. Processing of the crime scene

Law enforcement personnel and other non-medical investigators should co-ordinate their efforts in processing the scene with those of medical personnel. Persons conducting an investigation should have access to the scene where the body was discovered and to the scene where the death may have occurred:

(a) The area around the body should be closed off. Only investigators and their staff should be allowed entry into the area;

(b) Colour photographs of the victim should be taken as these, in comparison with black and white photographs, may reveal in more detail the nature and circumstances of the victim's death;

(c) Photographs should be taken of the scene (interior and exterior) and of any other physical evidence;

146

(d) A record should be made of the body position and condition of the clothing;

(e) The following factors may be helpful in estimating the time of death:

(i) Temperature of the body (warm, cool, cold);

(ii) Location and degree of fixation of lividity;

(iii) Rigidity of the body;

(iv) Stage of its decomposition;

(f) Examination of the scene for blood should take place. Any samples of blood, hair, fibres and threads should be collected and preserved;

(g) If the victim appears to have been sexually assaulted, this fact should be recorded;

(h) A record should be made of any vehicles found in the area;

(i) Castings should be made and preserved of pry marks, tyre or shoe impressions, or any other impressions of an evidentiary nature;

(j) Any evidence of weapons, such as guns, projectiles, bullets and cartridge cases, should be taken and preserved. When applicable, tests for gunshot residue and trace metal detection should be performed;

(k) Any fingerprints should be located, developed, lifted and preserved;

(l) A sketch of the crime scene to scale should be made showing all relevant details of the crime, such as the location of weapons, furniture, vehicles, surrounding terrain, including the position, height and width of items, and their relationship to each other;

(m) A record of the identity of all persons at the scene should be made, including complete names, addresses and telephone numbers;

(n) Information should be obtained from scene witnesses, including those who last saw the decedent alive, when, where and under what circumstances;

(o) Any relevant papers, records or documents should be saved for evidentiary use and handwriting analysis.

2. Processing of the evidence

(a) The body must be identified by reliable witnesses and other objective methods;

(b) A report should be made detailing any observations at the scene, actions of investigators and disposition of all evidence recovered;

(c) Property forms listing all evidence should be completed;

(d) Evidence must be properly collected, handled, packaged, labelled and placed in safekeeping to prevent contamination and loss of evidence.

147

3. Avenues to investigation

(a) What evidence is there, if any, that the death was premeditated and intentional, rather than accidental? Is there any evidence of torture?

(b) What weapon or means was used and in what manner?

(c) How many persons were involved in the death?

(d) What other crime, if any, and the exact details thereof, was committed during or associated with the death?

(e) What was the relationship between the suspected perpetrator(s) and the victim prior to the death?

(f) Was the victim a member of any political, religious, ethnic or social group(s), and could this have been a motive for the death?

4. Personal testimony

(a) Investigators should identify and interview all potential witnesses to the crime, including:

(i) Suspects;

(ii) Relatives and friends of the victim;

(iii) Persons who knew the victim;

(iv) Individuals residing or located in the area of the crime;

(v) Persons who knew or had knowledge of the suspects;

(vi) Persons who may have observed either the crime, the scene, the victim or the suspects in the week prior to the execution;

(vii) Persons having knowledge of possible motives;

(b) Interviews should take place as soon as possible and should be written and/or taped. All tapes should be transcribed and maintained;

(c) Witnesses should be interviewed individually, and assurance should be given that any possible means of protecting their safety before, during and after the proceedings will be used, if necessary.

D. Commission of inquiry

In cases where government involvement is suspected, an objective and impartial investigation may not be possible unless a special commission of inquiry is established. A commission of inquiry may also be necessary where the expertise of the investigators is called into question. This section sets out factors that give rise to a presumption of government complicity, partiality or insufficient expertise on the part of those conducting the investigation. Any one of these presumptions should trigger the creation of a special commission of inquiry. It then sets out procedures that can be used as a model for the creation and function of commissions of inquiry. The procedures were derived from the experience of major inquiries that have been mounted to investigate executions or similarly grievous cases of human rights violations.

Establishing a commission of inquiry entails defining the scope of the inquiry, appointing commission members and staff, determining the type of proceedings to be followed and selecting procedures governing those proceedings, and authorizing the commission to report on its findings and make recommendations. Each of these areas will be covered separately.

1. Factors triggering a special investigation

Factors that support a belief that the Government was involved in the execution, and that should trigger the creation of a special impartial investigation commission include:

(a) Where the political views, religious or ethnic affiliation, or social status of the victim give rise to a suspicion of government involvement or complicity in the death because of any one or combination of the following factors:

(i) Where the victim was last seen alive in police custody or detention;

(ii) Where the modus operandi is recognizably attributable to government-sponsored death squads;

(iii) Where persons in the Government or associated with the Government have attempted to obstruct or delay the investigation of the execution;

(iv) Where the physical or testimonial evidence essential to the investigation becomes unavailable.

(b) As set out in paragraph 11 of the Principles, an independent commission of inquiry or similar procedure should also be established where a routine investigation is inadequate for the following reasons:

(i) The lack of expertise; or

(ii) The lack of impartiality; or

(iii) The importance of the matter; or

(iv) The apparent existence of a pattern of abuse; or

(v) Complaints from the family of the victim about the above inadequacies or other substantial reasons.

2. Defining the scope of the inquiry

Governments and organizations establishing commissions of inquiry need to define the scope of the inquiry by including terms of reference in their authorization. Defining the commission's terms of reference can greatly increase its success by giving legitimacy to the proceedings, assisting commission members in reaching a consensus on the scope of inquiry and providing a measure by which the commission's final report can be judged. Recommendations for defining terms of reference are as follows:

(a) They should be neutrally framed so that they do not suggest a predetermined outcome. To be neutral, terms of reference must not limit investigations in areas that might uncover government responsibility for extra-legal, arbitrary and summary executions;

149

(b) They should state precisely which events and issues are to be investigated and addressed in the commission's final report;

(c) They should provide flexibility in the scope of inquiry to ensure that thorough investigation by the commission is not hampered by overly restrictive or overly broad terms of reference. The necessary flexibility may be accomplished, for example by permitting the commission to amend its terms of reference as necessary. It is important, however, that the commission keep the public informed of any amendments to its charge.

3. Power of the commission

The principles set out in a general manner the powers of the commission. More specifically such a commission would need the following:

(a) To have the authority to obtain all information necessary to the inquiry, for example, for determining the cause, manner and time of death, including the authority to compel testimony under legal sanction, to order the production of documents including government and medical records, and to protect witnesses, families of the victim and other sources;

(b) To have the authority to issue a public report;

(c) To have the authority to prevent the burial or other disposal of the body until an adequate postmortem examination has been performed;

(d) To have the authority to conduct on-site visits, both at the scene where the body was discovered and at the scene where the death may have occurred;

(e) To have the authority to receive evidence from witnesses and organizations located outside the country.

4. Membership qualifications

Commission members should be chosen for their recognized impartiality, competence and independence as individuals:

Impartiality. Commission members should not be closely associated with any individual, government entity, political party or other organization potentially implicated in the execution or disappearance, or an organization or group associated with the victim, as this may damage the commission's credibility.

Competence. Commission members must be capable of evaluating and weighing evidence, and exercising sound judgement. If possible, commissions of inquiry should include individuals with expertise in law, medicine, forensic science and other specialized fields, as appropriate.

Independence. Members of the commission should have a reputation in their community for honesty and fairness.

5. Number of commissioners

The Principles do not contain a provision on the number of members of the commission, but it would not be unreasonable to note that objectivity of the investigation and commission's findings may, among other things, depend on whether it has three or more members rather than one or two. Investigations

150

into extra-legal, arbitrary and summary executions should, in general, not be conducted by a single commissioner. A single, isolated commissioner will generally be limited in the depth of investigation he or she can conduct alone. In addition, a single commissioner will have to make controversial and important decisions without debate, and will be particularly vulnerable to governmental and other outside pressure.

6. Choosing a commission counsel

Commissions of inquiry should have impartial, expert counsel. Where the commission is investigating allegations of governmental misconduct, it would be advisable to appoint counsel outside the Ministry of Justice. The chief counsel to the commission should be insulated from political influence, as through civil service tenure, or status as a wholly independent member of the bar.

7. Choosing expert advisors

The investigation will often require expert advisors. Technical expertise in such areas as pathology, forensic science and ballistics should be available to the commission.

8. Choosing investigators

To conduct a completely impartial and thorough investigation, the commission will almost always need its own investigators to pursue leads and to develop evidence. The credibility of an inquiry will be significantly enhanced to the extent that the commission can rely on its own investigators.

9. Protection of witnesses

(a) The Government shall protect complainants, witnesses, those conducting the investigation, and their families from violence, threats of violence or any other form of intimidation;

(b) If the commission concludes that there is a reasonable fear of persecution, harassment, or harm to any witness or prospective witness, the commission may find it advisable:

    (i) To hear the evidence in camera;

    (ii) To keep the identity of the informant or witness confidential;

    (iii) To use only such evidence as will not present a risk of identifying the witness;

    (iv) To take any other appropriate measures.

10. Proceedings

It follows from general principles of criminal procedure that hearings should be conducted in public, unless in camera proceedings are necessary to protect the safety of a witness. In camera proceedings should be recorded and the closed, unpublished record kept in a known location.

Occasionally, complete secrecy may be required to encourage testimony, and the commission will want to hear witnesses privately, informally and without recording testimony.

11. Notice of inquiry

Wide notice of the establishment of a commission and the subject of the
inquiry should be given. The notice should also include an invitation to
submit relevant information and/or written statements to the commission, and
instructions to persons wishing to testify. Notice can be disseminated
through newspapers, magazines, radio, television, leaflets and posters.

12. Receipt of evidence

Power to compel evidence. As emphasized in Principle 10 (see annex I),
commissions of inquiry should have the power to compel testimony and production
of documents: in this context, Principle 10 refers to "the authority to oblige
officials" allegedly involved in extra-legal, arbitrary and summary executions.
Practically, this authority may involve the power to impose fines or sentences
if the Government or individuals refuse to comply.

Use of witness statements. Commissions of inquiry should invite persons
to testify or submit written statements as a first step in gathering evidence.
Written statements may become an important source of evidence if their authors
become afraid to testify, cannot travel to proceedings, or are otherwise
unavailable.

Use of evidence from other proceedings. Commissions of inquiry should
review other proceedings that could provide relevant information. For example,
the commission should obtain the findings from an inquest into cause of death,
conducted by a coroner or medical examiner. Such inquests generally rely on
postmortem or autopsy examinations. A commission of inquiry should review the
inquest and the results of the autopsy presented to the inquest to determine
if they were conducted thoroughly and impartially. If the inquest and autopsy
were so conducted, the coroner's findings are entitled to be given great
weight.

13. Rights of parties

As mentioned in Principle 16, families of the deceased and their legal
representatives shall be informed of, and have access to, any hearing and to
all information relevant to the investigation, and shall be entitled to
present evidence. This particular emphasis on the role of the family as a
party to the proceedings implies the specially important role the family's
interests play in the conduct of the investigation. However, all other
interested parties should also have the opportunity at being heard. As mentioned in Principle 10, the investigative body shall be entitled to issue
summons to witnesses, including the officials allegedly involved and to demand
the production of evidence. All these witnesses should be permitted legal
counsel if they are likely to be harmed by the inquiry, for example, when
their testimony could expose them to criminal charges or civil liability.
Witnesses may not be compelled to testify against themselves regarding matters
unrelated to the scope of inquiry.

There should be an opportunity for the effective questioning of witnesses
by the commission. Parties to the inquiry should be allowed to submit written
questions to the commission.

14. Evaluation of evidence

The commission shall assess all information and evidence it receives to
determine its relevance, veracity, reliability and probity. The commission

Enrique Pérez López, President of the South-South Eastern Human
Rights Association of Comitán, was abducted on April 10 by heavily
armed ranchers near Chicomuselo due to a land dispute. The ranchers
reportedly beat Pérez and handed him over to police who charged him
with destruction of property. Unable to post bail, Pérez was taken to
Prison No. 10 in Comitán. On May 16, with Pérez's encouragement, 38
prisoners held a hunger strike at Comitán prison. On the third day of the
strike Pérez was released and, within several weeks, the other detainees
were released. (See Chapter V.)

Sebastián Santiz López

Hermelindo Santiz Gómez

Sebastián Santiz López, Hermelindo Santiz Gómez, and a third man, Severiano Santiz Gómez, were last seen alive in the custody of Mexican soldiers in the ejido of Morelia on January 7, 1994 (see Chapter VI). According to residents of Morelia, the three men were tortured by Mexican soldiers in the village church (above).

PHR consultants Clyde Collins Snow (left) and Thomas Crane, M.D. (center), along with a member of the National Commission on Human Rights (CNDH), examine skeletal remains which they later identified as those of the three men who were abducted by Mexican soldiers in Morelia.

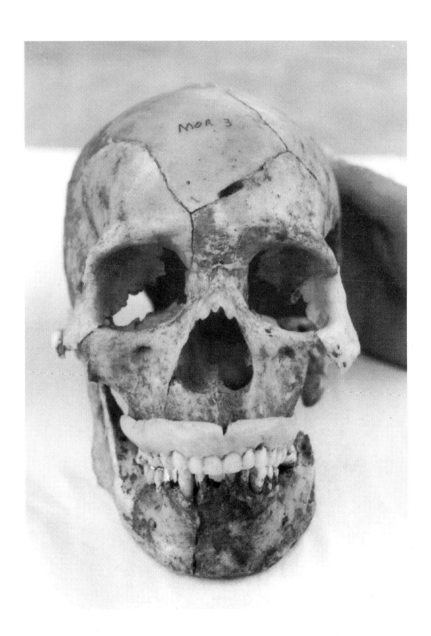

The reconstructed skull of Sebastián Santiz López.

Four persons were killed when Mexican army troops opened fire on a small passenger bus, known as a "Combi," which had failed to stop at an army checkpoint in Rancho Nuevo.
(credit: *La Jornada*-Carlos Cisneros)

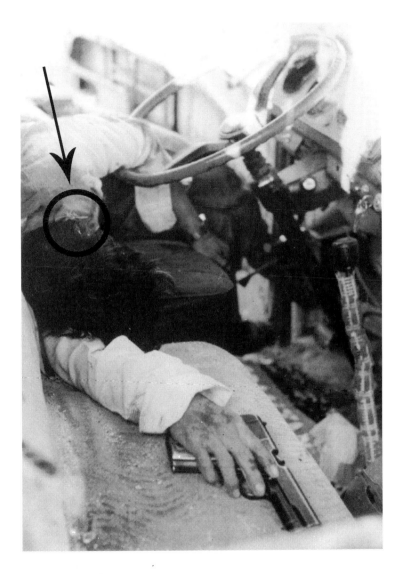

The Mexican army claims that this passenger was armed and died in the position shown in the photograph. However, the position of the body and the fact that there are tufts of grass in the man's hair and clothing (circled) suggest that the body had been removed from the Combi and deliberately placed in this position for the photograph.

(credit: *La Jornada*- Carlos Cisneros)

A CASE OF MISIDENTIFICATION

A

On January 4, 1994, after intense fighting between Mexican army troops and EZLN rebels, reporters counted over forty bodies laying in the streets of Ocosingo (see Chapter VI). In the town marketplace, they found the bodies of five men, dressed in rebel uniforms and lying face down next to a market stall (photo A). The bodies appeared to have been bound with ligatures and exhibited close range gunshot wounds to the head. (Credit: *La Jornada*-Raúl Ortega)

B

In a separate incident, two days earlier, on January 2, 1994, two
civilians from the town of Oxchuc--Pablo Santiz Gómez and his son,
Uber--transported a group of EZLN rebels in their minibus to the nearby
village of Huixtan (see Chapter V). The following day, journalists
discovered the bullet-ridden minibus on the side of the road near the
army base of Rancho Nuevo (photo B). About seven meters from the
vehicle lay the bodies of fourteen men.
(Credit: *La Jornada*- Fabrizio León)

When investigators with the federal Attorney General's office
(*Procuraduría General de la República/PGR*) showed photographs of the
scene to Pablo Santiz Gómez's wife, she identified her husband (see
photo C) and son (photo D) among the dead.

C - Pablo Santiz Gómez

D - Uber Santiz Gómez

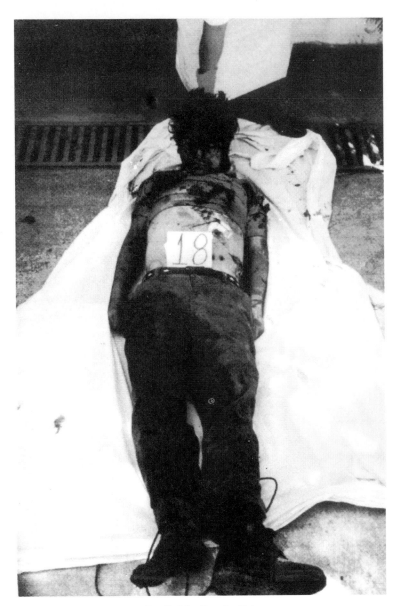

E - Pablo Santiz Gómez

She also identified them from autopsy photographs (photo E). Death certificates were then issued giving the place of death for both men as "along the stretch of road between San Cristóbal and Oxchuc" (photos F,G).

In a press statement dated April 7, the PGR ruled out any military involvement in the summary executions of the five men in the Ocosingo marketplace. Army troops, the agency said, were not in the vicinity of the marketplace at the time the killings occurred--a fact which is contradicted by press reports at the time. The PGR also announced that its forensic experts had identified two of the five men as civilians--one of whom was a bus driver from the town of Oxchuc named Pablo Santiz Gómez.

ESTADOS UNIDOS MEXICANOS
REGISTRO CIVIL

04171

BOLETA No. 4151887 FECHA 08-03-94 DERECHOS N$ 16.00 1/2

EN NOMBRE DEL ESTADO LIBRE Y SOBERANO DE _____ C H I A P A S _____
Y COMO OFICIAL _____ 01 _____ DEL REGISTRO CIVIL DE ESTA JURISDICCION
CERTIFICO: QUE EN EL LIBRO No. _____ 01 _____ DEL REGISTRO CIVIL QUE ES A MI CARGO.
EN LA FOJA No. 03665 SE ENCUENTRA ASENTADA EL ACTA No. 060 DE FECHA:
23 DE FEBRERO DE 1994. LEVANTADA POR EL C. OFICIAL 01
DEL REGISTRO CIVIL LIC. DELINA ANTONIETA MONTESINOS PAREDES.
EN LA CUAL SE CONTIENEN LOS SIGUIENTES DATOS:

ACTA DE DEFUNCION
FINADO (A)
NOMBRE PABLO SANTIZ GOMEZ. SEXO: MASCULINO (X) FEMENINO ( )
ESTADO CIVIL CASADO NACIONALIDAD - - - - - - - EDAD 35 AÑOS
FECHA DE NACIMIENTO - - - - - - - - -
LUGAR DE NACIMIENTO PARAJE SANTISIMA TRINIDAD, MPIO. DE OXCHUC, CHIAPAS.
NOMBRE DEL CONYUGE - - - - - - - - - - NACIONALIDAD - - - - - -
NOMBRE DEL PADRE MATEO SANTIZ GOMEZ. (FINADO) NACIONALIDAD - - - - - -
NOMBRE DE LA MADRE CANDELARIA GOMEZ LOPEZ. NACIONALIDAD - - - - - -
DESTINO DEL CADAVER: INHUMACION (X) CREMACION ( )
NOMBRE DEL PANTEON O CREMATORIO - - - - - - - - -
UBICACION TUXTLA GUTIERREZ, CHIAPAS.
FALLECIMIENTO
FECHA DE LA DEFUNCION: DIA - - MES - - - - - - - AÑO - - HORA - - - -
LUGAR CARRETERA TRAMO SAN CRISTOBAL-OXCHUC.
CAUSA(S) DE LA MUERTE CONSECUENCIA DE SHOCK NEUROGENICO Y SHOCK HIPOVOLEMI CO AGUDO SECUNDARIOS A LAS LESIONES DE MASA ENCEFALICA Y DE VICERA INTRETARACICA CAUSADOS POR PROYECTIL DE ARMA DE FUEGO. - - - - -
NOMBRE DEL MEDICO QUE CERTIFICO LA DEFUNCION No. DE CEDULA PROFESIONAL No. DE CERTIFICADO - - - - - -

DECLARANTE
NOMBRE MATEO SANTIZ GOMEZ. EDAD 38 AÑOS
NACIONALIDAD MEXICANA PARENTESCO HERMANO
TESTIGOS
NOMBRE CARLOS SANCHEZ VAZQUEZ. EDAD 24 AÑOS
NACIONALIDAD MEXICANA PARENTESCO TIO
NOMBRE VIRGILIO AGUILAR CALVA. EDAD 34 AÑOS
NACIONALIDAD MEXICANA PARENTESCO NINGUNO

SE EXTIENDE ESTA CERTIFICACION, EN CUMPLIMIENTO DEL ARTICULO 45 DEL CODIGO CIVIL VIGENTE EN EL ESTADO, EN TUXTLA GUTIERREZ, CHIAPAS. A LOS 08 DIAS DEL MES DE MARZO DE 1994.
EL C. OFICIAL 01 DEL REGISTRO CIVIL, DOY FE
cotejo
mdm.
LIC. DELINA ANTONIETA MONTESINOS PAREDES.
NOMBRE FIRMA

F - Death certificate: Pablo Santiz Gómez

In April 1994, Physicians for Human Rights (PHR) and Human Rights Watch/Americas (HRW/Americas) sent letters to the PGR and the National Commission of Human Rights pointing out the contradictions and omissions of fact in the PGR's bulletin and criticizing its exoneration of army personnel from any possible involvement in the Ocosingo killings. So far, neither agency has responded to these queries.

HRW/Americas and PHR have called on the Mexican government to appoint immediately an independent, special commission of inquiry to investigate the five killings in the Ocosingo marketplace and the manner in which the PGR has handled its own investigation of the case.

ESTADOS UNIDOS MEXICANOS
REGISTRO CIVIL

No DE CONTROL VI-OCO 949
04162

BOLETA No Art. 132 FECHA Ley Hac. DERECHOS - - - 1/1

EN NOMBRE DEL ESTADO LIBRE Y SOBERANO DE _____ C H I A P A S
Y COMO OFICIAL _____ 01 _____ DEL REGISTRO CIVIL DE ESTA JURISDICCION
CERTIFICO: QUE EN EL LIBRO No 03666 01 _____ DEL REGISTRO CIVIL QUE ES A MI CARGO
EN LA FOJA No. _____ SE ENCUENTRA ASENTADA EL ACTA No _____ 061 _____ DE FECHA
23 DE FEBRERO DE 1994, LEVANTADA POR EL C. OFICIAL _____ 01
DEL REGISTRO CIVIL _____ LIC. DELINA ANTONIETA MONTESINOS PAREDES.
EN LA CUAL SE CONTIENEN LOS SIGUIENTES DATOS:

ACTA DE DEFUNCION
FINADO (A)

NOMBRE UBER SANTIZ GOMEZ. SEXO: MASCULINO (X) FEMENINO ◯
ESTADO CIVIL UNION LIBRE NACIONALIDAD _____ EDAD 17 ANOS
FECHA DE NACIMIENTO _____
LUGAR DE NACIMIENTO PARAJE SANTISIMA TRINIDAD, OXCHUC.
NOMBRE DEL CONYUGE _____ NACIONALIDAD _____
NOMBRE DEL PADRE PABLO SANTIZ GOMEZ, (FINADO) NACIONALIDAD _____
NOMBRE DE LA MADRE ANA GOMEZ SANTIZ. NACIONALIDAD _____
DESTINO DEL CADAVER: INHUMACION (X) CREMACION ◯
NOMBRE DEL PANTEON O CREMATORIO _____
UBICACION TUXTLA GUTIERREZ, CHIAPAS.

FALLECIMIENTO

FECHA DE LA DEFUNCION _____ MES _____ AÑO _____ HORA _____
LUGAR TRAMO CARRETERA SAN CRISTOBAL-OXCHUC.
CAUSAS(S) DE LA MUERTE SHOCK NEUROGENICO Y HEMORRAGIA CEREBRAL AGUDA POR DES
TRUCCION DE MASA ENCEFALICA PRODUCIDO POR PROYECTIL DE ARMA DE FUE
GO.

NOMBRE DEL MEDICO QUE CERTIFICO LA DEFUNCION. No. DE CEDULA PROFESIONAL No DE CERTIFICADO

DECLARANTE

NOMBRE MATEO SANTIZ GOMEZ. EDAD 38 ANOS
NACIONALIDAD MEXICANA PARENTESCO - TIO

TESTIGOS

NOMBRE CARLOS SANCHEZ VAZQUEZ. EDAD 24 ANOS
NACIONALIDAD MEXICANA PARENTESCO TIO
NOMBRE VIRGILIO AGUILAR CALVA. EDAD 34 ANOS
NACIONALIDAD MEXICANA PARENTESCO NINGUNO

SE EXTIENDE ESTA CERTIFICACION EN LA CIUDAD DE TUXTLA GUTIERREZ, CHIAPAS, DEL
CODIGO CIVIL VIGENTE EN EL ESTADO, EN _____ 45
A LOS 04 DIAS DEL MES DE MARZO DE 1994.
EL C OFICIAL 01 DEL REGISTRO CIVIL DON EL _____ SELLO

cotejo
mdm.

LIC. DELINA ANTONIETA MONTESINOS PAREDES.

G - Death Certificate: Uber Santiz Gómez

Personnel from the National Commission on Human Rights exhume eleven bodies from a common grave in the Ocosingo cemetery. Nine of the bodies were later identified as civilians; some of whom are believed to have been killed during the occupation of the Ocosingo hospital by Mexican army troops on January 3, 1994. At least two of the deceased were last seen alive in the custody of Mexican soldiers.

(Credit: *Síntesis: La Guerra de los Olvidados*)

Mexican army troops drill in front of the San Carlos Hospital in Altamirano.

should evaluate oral testimony based upon the demeanour and overall credibility of the witness. Corroboration of evidence from several sources will increase the probative value of such evidence. The reliability of hearsay evidence from several sources will increase the probative value of such evidence. The reliability of hearsay evidence must be considered carefully before the commission should accept it as fact. Testimony not tested by cross-examination must also be viewed with caution. In camera testimony preserved in a closed record or not recorded at all is often not subjected to cross-examination and therefore may be given less weight.

15. The report of the commission

As stated in Principle 17, the commission should issue a public report within a reasonable period of time. It may be added that where the commission is not unanimous in its findings, the minority commissioner(s) should file a dissenting opinion.

From the practical experience gathered, commission of inquiry reports should contain the following information:

(a) The scope of inquiry and terms of reference;

(b) The procedures and methods of evaluating evidence;

(c) A list of all witnesses who have testified, except for those whose identities are withheld for protection and who have testified in camera, and exhibits received in evidence;

(d) The time and place of each sitting (this might be annexed to the report);

(e) The background to the inquiry such as relevant social, political and economic conditions;

(f) The specific events that occurred and the evidence upon which such findings are based;

(g) The law upon which the commission relied;

(h) The commission's conclusions based upon applicable law and findings of fact;

(i) Recommendations based upon the findings of the commission.

16. Response of the Government

The Government should either reply publicly to the commission's report or should indicate what steps it intends to take in response to the report.

153

PRINCIPLES ON THE EFFECTIVE PREVENTION AND INVESTIGATION OF EXTRA-LEGAL, ARBITRARY AND SUMMARY EXECUTIONS

Effective prevention and investigation of extra-legal, arbitrary and summary executions

The Economic and Social Council,*

Recalling that article 3 of the Universal Declaration of Human Rights a/ [108] proclaims that everyone has the right to life, liberty and security of person,

Bearing in mind that paragraph 1 of article 6 of the International Covenant on Civil and Political Rights b/ [114] states that every human being has an inherent right to life, that that right shall be protected by law and that no one shall be arbitrarily deprived of his or her life,

Also bearing in mind the general comments of the Human Rights Committee on the right to life as enunciated in article 6 of the International Covenant on Civil and Political Rights,

Stressing that extra-legal, arbitrary and summary executions contravene the human rights and fundamental freedoms proclaimed in the Universal Declaration of Human Rights,

Mindful that the Seventh United Nations Congress on the Prevention of Crime and the Treatment of Offenders, in resolution 11 on extra-legal, arbitrary and summary executions, c/ [93] called upon all Governments to take urgent and incisive action to investigate such acts, wherever they may occur, to punish those found guilty and to take all other measures necessary to prevent those practices,

Mindful also that the Economic and Social Council, in section VI of its resolution 1986/10 of 21 May 1986, requested the Committee on Crime Prevention and Control to consider at its tenth session the question of extra-legal, arbitrary and summary executions with a view to elaborating principles on the effective prevention and investigation of such practices,

Recalling that the General Assembly in its resolution 33/173 of 20 December 1978 expressed its deep concern at reports from various parts of the world relating to enforced or involuntary disappearances and called upon Governments, in the event of such reports, to take appropriate measures to searching for such persons and to undertake speedy and impartial investigations,

Noting with appreciation the efforts of non-governmental organizations to develop standards for investigations, d/ [115]

Note: References are numbered a/, b/ etc., with the original numbering from the resolution given in square brackets immediately following the footnote indicators.

*Resolution 1989/65 of 24 May 1989.

Emphasizing that the General Assembly in its resolution 42/141 of
7 December 1987 strongly condemned once again the large number of summary or
arbitrary executions, including extra-legal executions, that continued to take
place in various parts of the world,

Noting that in the same resolution the General Assembly recognized the
need for closer co-operation between the Centre for Human Rights, the Crime
Prevention and Criminal Justice Branch of the Centre for Social Development
and Humanitarian Affairs and the Committee on Crime Prevention and Control in
an effort to bring to an end summary or arbitrary executions,

Aware that effective prevention and investigation of extra-legal,
arbitrary and summary executions requires the provision of adequate financial
and technical resources,

1. Recommends that the Principles on the Effective Prevention and
Investigation of Extra-legal, Arbitrary and Summary Executions annexed to the
present resolution shall be taken into account and respected by Governments
within the framework of their national legislation and practices, and shall be
brought to the attention of law enforcement and criminal justice officials,
military personnel, lawyers, members of the executive and legislative bodies
of the Government and the public in general;

2. Requests the Committee on Crime Prevention and Control to keep the
above recommendations under constant review, including implementation of the
Principles, taking into account the various socio-economic, political and
cultural circumstances in which extra-legal, arbitrary and summary executions
occur;

3. Invites Member States that have not yet ratified or acceded to international instruments that prohibit extra-legal, arbitrary and summary executions, including the International Covenant on Civil and Political Rights, b/
[114] the Optional Protocol to the International Covenant on Civil and
Political Rights and the Convention against Torture and Other Cruel, Inhuman
or Degrading Treatment or Punishment, e/ [116] to become parties to these
instruments;

4. Requests the Secretary-General to include the Principles in the
United Nations publication entitled Human Rights: A Compilation of International Instruments;

5. Requests the United Nations regional and interregional institutes for
the prevention of crime and the treatment of offenders to give special attention in their research and training programmes to the Principles, and to the
International Covenant on Civil and Political Rights, b/ [114] the provisions
of the Convention against Torture and Other Cruel, Inhuman or Degrading
Treatment or Punishment, e/ [116] the Code of Conduct for Law Enforcement
Officials, f/ [104] the Declaration of Basic Principles of Justice for Victims
of Crime and Abuse of Power g/ [102] and other international instruments
relevant to the question of extra-legal, arbitrary and summary executions.

PRINCIPLES ON THE EFFECTIVE PREVENTION AND INVESTIGATION OF EXTRA-LEGAL, ARBITRARY AND SUMMARY EXECUTIONS

Prevention

1. Governments shall prohibit by law all extra-legal, arbitrary and summary executions and shall ensure that any such executions are recognized as offences under their criminal laws, and are punishable by appropriate penalties which take into account the seriousness of such offences. Exceptional circumstances including a state of war or threat of war, internal political instability or any other public emergency may not be invoked as a justification of such executions. Such executions shall not be carried out under any circumstances including, but not limited to, situations of internal armed conflict, excessive or illegal use of force by a public official or other person acting in an official capacity or a person acting at the instigation, or with the consent or acquiescence of such person, and situations in which deaths occur in custody. This prohibition shall prevail over decrees issued by governmental authority.

2. In order to prevent extra-legal, arbitrary and summary executions, Governments shall ensure strict control, including a clear chain of command over all officials responsible for the apprehension, arrest, detention, custody and imprisonment as well as those officials authorized by law to use force and firearms.

3. Governments shall prohibit orders from superior officers or public authorities authorizing or inciting other persons to carry out any such extra-legal, arbitrary or summary executions. All persons shall have the right and the duty to defy such orders. Training of law enforcement officials shall emphasize the above provisions.

4. Effective protection through judicial or other means shall be guaranteed to individuals and groups who are in danger of extra-legal, arbitrary or summary executions, including those who receive death threats.

5. No one shall be involuntarily returned or extradited to a country where there are substantial grounds for believing that he or she may become a victim of extra-legal, arbitrary or summary execution in that country.

6. Governments shall ensure that persons deprived of their liberty are held in officially recognized places of custody, and that accurate information on their custody and whereabouts, including transfers, is made promptly available to their relatives and lawyer or other persons of confidence.

7. Qualified inspectors, including medical personnel, or an equivalent independent authority, shall conduct inspections in places of custody on a regular basis, and be empowered to undertake unannounced inspections on their own initiative, with full guarantees of independence in the exercise of this function. The inspectors shall have unrestricted access to all persons in such places of custody, as well as to all their records.

8. Governments shall make every effort to prevent extra-legal, arbitrary and summary executions through measures such as diplomatic intercession, improved access of complainants to intergovernmental and judicial bodies, and public denunciation. Intergovernmental mechanisms shall be used to investigate reports of any such executions and to take effective action against such

practices. Governments, including those of countries where extra-legal, arbitrary and summary executions are reasonably suspected to occur, shall co-operate fully in international investigations on the subject.

Investigation

9. There shall be a thorough, prompt and impartial investigation of all suspected cases of extra-legal, arbitrary and summary executions, including cases where complaints by relatives or other reliable reports suggest unnatural death in the above circumstances. Governments shall maintain investigative offices and procedures to undertake such inquiries. The purpose of the investigation shall be to determine the cause, manner and time of death, the person responsible, and any adequate autopsy, collection and analysis of all physical and documentary evidence, and statements from witnesses. The investigation shall distinguish between natural death, accidental death, suicide and homicide.

10. The investigative authority shall have the power to obtain all the information necessary to the inquiry. Those persons conducting the investigation shall have at their disposal all the necessary budgetary and technical resources for effective investigation. They shall also have the authority to oblige officials allegedly involved in any such executions to appear and testify. The same shall apply to any witness. To this end, they shall be entitled to issue summons to witnesses, including the officials allegedly involved, and to demand the production of evidence.

11. In cases in which the established investigative procedures are inadequate because of lack of expertise or impartiality, because of the importance of the matter or because of the apparent existence of a pattern of abuse, and in cases where there are complaints from the family of the victim about these inadequacies or other substantial reasons, Governments shall pursue investigations through an independent commission of inquiry or similar procedure. Members of such a commission shall be chosen for their recognized impartiality, competence and independence as individuals. In particular, they shall be independent of any institution, agency or person that may be the subject of the inquiry. The commission shall have the authority to obtain all information necessary to the inquiry and shall conduct the inquiry as provided for under these Principles.

12. The body of the deceased person shall not be disposed of until an adequate autopsy is conducted by a physician, who shall, if possible, be an expert in forensic pathology. Those conducting the autopsy shall have the right of access to all investigative data, to the place where the body was discovered, and to the place where the death is thought to have occurred. If the body has been buried and it later appears that an investigation is required, the body shall be promptly and competently exhumed for an autopsy. If skeletal remains are discovered, they should be carefully exhumed and studied according to systematic anthropological techniques.

13. The body of the deceased shall be available to those conducting the autopsy for a sufficient amount of time to enable a thorough investigation to be carried out. The autopsy shall, at a minimum, attempt to establish the identity of the deceased and the cause and manner of death. The time and place of death shall also be determined to the extent possible. Detailed colour photographs of the deceased shall be included in the autopsy report in order to document and support the findings of the investigation. The autopsy report must describe any and all injuries to the deceased including any evidence of torture.

14. In order to ensure objective results, those conducting the autopsy must be able to function impartially and independently of any potentially implicated persons or organizations or entities.

15. Complainants, witnesses, those conducting the investigation and their families shall be protected from violence, threats of violence or any other form of intimidation. Those potentially implicated in extra-legal, arbitrary or summary executions shall be removed from any position of control or power, whether direct or indirect, over complainants, witnesses and their families, as well as over those conducting investigations.

16. Families of the deceased and their legal representatives shall be informed of, and have access to, any hearing as well as to all information relevant to the investigation, and shall be entitled to present other evidence. The family of the deceased shall have the right to insist that a medical or other qualified representative be present at the autopsy. When the identity of a deceased person has been determined, a notification of death shall be posted, and the family or relatives of the deceased immediately informed. The body of the deceased shall be returned to them upon completion of the investigation.

17. A written report shall be made within a reasonable period of time on the methods and findings of such investigations. The report shall be made public immediately and shall include the scope of the inquiry, procedures and methods used to evaluate evidence as well as conclusions and recommendations based on findings of fact and on applicable law. The report shall also describe in detail specific events that were found to have occurred, and the evidence upon which such findings were based, and list the names of witnesses who testified, with the exception of those whose identities have been withheld for their own protection. The Government shall, within a reasonable period of time, either reply to the report of the investigation, or indicate the steps to be taken in response to it.

Legal proceedings

18. Governments shall ensure that persons identified by the investigation as having participated in extra-legal, arbitrary and summary executions in any territory under their jurisdiction are brought to justice. Governments shall either bring such persons to justice or co-operate to extradite any such persons to other countries wishing to exercise jurisdiction. This principle shall apply irrespective of who and where the perpetrators or the victims are, their nationalities or where the offence was committed.

19. Without prejudice to Principle 3 above, an order from a superior officer or a public authority may not be invoked as a justification for extra-legal, arbitrary or summary executions. Superiors, officers or other public officials may be held responsible for acts committed by officials under their hierarchical authority if they had a reasonable opportunity to prevent such acts. In no circumstances, including a state of war, siege or other public emergency, shall blanket immunity from prosecution be granted to any person allegedly involved in extra-legal, arbitrary or summary executions.

20. The families and dependents of victims of extra-legal, arbitrary and summary executions shall be entitled to fair and adequate compensation within a reasonable period of time.

Notes

a/ General Assembly resolution 217 A (III).

b/ See General Assembly resolution 2200 A (XXI), annex.

c/ See <u>Seventh United Nations Congress on the Prevention of Crime and the Treatment of Offenders, Milan, 26 August–6 September 1985: report prepared by the Secretariat</u> (United Nations publication, Sales No. E.86.IV.1) chap. I, sect. E.

d/ See E/AC.57/1988/NGO.4.

e/ General Assembly resolution 39/46, annex.

f/ General Assembly resolution 34/169, annex.

g/ General Assembly resolution 40/34, annex.